J84

J84

A Guide for
Collectors of Folklore
in Utah

Volume seven of the University of Utah Publications in the
American West, under the editorial direction of the
Center for Studies of the American West,
Don D. Walker, Chairman, Editorial Board.

Published in cooperation with the Utah Heritage Foundation.

University of Utah Press
Salt Lake City, Utah

A Guide for Collectors of Folklore in Utah

Jan Harold Brunvand

Contents

Foreword

The culture of the folk is represented in the broad preservation programs of the Utah Heritage Foundation both by a working committee and by the membership of a specialist in folklore on its Advisory Council. This is as it should be, of course, since the folk of any society is the ultimate repository of patterns of behavior and the value system, and the point of departure for new cultures when the old ones have passed away.

Awareness of Utah's folk heritage has been in the minds of many individuals and many organized groups for a long time, though organizations have not always existed to channel this awareness into social action, and especially to articulate preservation activities in folk culture with those in history, architecture, archeology, natural resources, the natural environment, etc.

Already before World War I early editions of John A. Lomax's *Cowboy Songs* had reached Utah farms and ranches, and several enthusiastic readers had sent him other cowboy and western songs, some of which were incorporated in later editions. The 78-rpm record had made its appearance, spreading folksong texts throughout the Great Basin, and by the late twenties local and national radio stations were throbbing to the refrains of folk and western music. Shortly, from Salt Lake City, Slim Critchlow and the Utah Buckaroos were singing in living rooms from the Four Corners to Goose Creek.

It took the soul-shaking impact of the depression of the thirties, however, to turn significant numbers of Utah citizens, or Utah-reared scholars, toward the orderly study and preservation of the regional heritage. The impact given by those years is still felt in an enriched awareness of the first century of the state's cultural development. Wayland D. Hand began to collect superstitions, folk medical practices, and mining lore within the state. Hector Lee was having students in his English courses at the University of Utah write the reminiscences of their ancestors, and anecdotes of family life in the rural areas of the state. Later he was able through the auspices of the Rockefeller Foundation to found the now defunct Utah Humanities Research Foundation. The Daughters of Utah Pioneers, under the dynamic leadership of Kate B. Carter, had begun their program to memorialize the founders of our region. Vardis Fisher and Wallace Stegner acquired some insights into the folk culture of Utah, and used them in fictional and other works. The WPA organized a Utah Writers' Project to employ aspiring writers, with Dale Morgan as its director. These workers assembled an important body of folk anecdote and verse which has been preserved through the efforts of the Utah State Historical Society and the Archive of Folklore in the Library of Congress. Lester Hubbard, Thomas Cheney, and Austin and Alta Fife had already begun their field collecting, and Juanita Brooks was writing those significant historical studies which manifest so much sensitivity to the culture of the folk.

In the following two decades there were new and more professional developments. A group of folk-minded citizens founded the Utah Folklore Society, and elected Louis Zucker of the University of Utah as its first president. The Sons of Utah Pioneers, under the patronage of Horace Sorenson, began a program of nostalgic interest in virile aspects of Utah heritage and established Pioneer Village, which is of great interest to residents and to tourists who visit Utah. The Daughters of Utah Pioneers also intensified their efforts and expanded their resources, creating the imposing museum on Capitol Hill which gives attention to folk culture.

In the forties and fifties the three universities also began to give formal attention to the folk culture in their curricula and in their research programs. At Brigham Young University the program was under Thomas Cheney; at the University of Utah under Louis Zucker, Lester Hubbard, and Hector Lee; and more recently at Utah State University a program was begun through the leadership of Austin Fife. Finally, in the mid-sixties two professionally trained young folklorists have added their expertise to these programs: William A. Wilson at BYU and Jan H. Brunvand, author of this work, at the U of U.

Foreword

The Committee on Folk Culture of the Utah Heritage Foundation is, of course, happy that its parent organization should have deemed the folk culture sufficiently important to sponsor the preparation and publication of this volume, and to undertake as one of its earliest major efforts a study of a unique local example of folk architecture: a style of stone houses in northern Utah of unique simplicity and charm, built from the late 1860s and of which perhaps fifty specimens still survive. A comprehensive study is now underway which will culminate, hopefully, in a published volume, the accumulation of materials for an exhibit, and permanent preservation of one or more of the houses in a few communities, particularly in Willard.

It is the hope of the members of this committee that this Collector's Guide will serve to give dignity, vitality, and order to efforts to preserve the culture of the folk throughout the state. We recognize the importance of such efforts in all its dimensions, and we are confident that the Utah Heritage Foundation must play the central role in this important work so that our lives may be the richer for having thus acquired deeper and more sentient roots.

AUSTIN E. FIFE, FOR THE

COMMITTEE ON FOLK CULTURE:

JUANITA BROOKS

JAN HAROLD BRUNVAND (CHAIRMAN)

HELEN Z. PAPANIKOLAS

MARTHA SCHACK

DOROTHY VAN STIPRIIAN

WILLIAM A. WILSON

Acknowledgments

A number of institutions and individuals helped make this publication possible. The University of Utah supported the work by providing office and archival facilities as well as by allowing me freedom to experiment in my various folklore classes in the Department of English. The University Library staff, especially Mrs. Ruth Yeaman of Western Americana, facilitated the archiving of student projects. The Utah Heritage Foundation and Center for Studies of the American West provided financial and moral support for the project from the start. Floyd Garn Hatch, chairman of the Foundation's Advisory Council, Richard Thurman, director of the University of Utah Press, and Gary D. Forbush, director of the Foundation, were unfailingly helpful in numerous ways. Dr. Everett L. Cooley aided the project both through his role as president of the Utah Heritage Foundation and as curator of Western Americana for the University of Utah. Professor Austin E. Fife of Utah State University and Professor William A. Wilson of Brigham Young University lent their special folklore talents and insights in the initial planning as well as in the final stages of editing and revision. Bert Wilson and Doug Hill and others identified in the picture credits are to be thanked for the use of their photographs. I am grateful also to Keith Montague for his work in designing this volume. Most of all I have the sources themselves of Utah folklore quoted herein to thank, along with my many student-collectors who allowed their work to become part of the archive.

J.H.B.

A Guide for
Collectors of Folklore
in Utah

Part One

Collecting Folklore in Utah

1

Folklore and Its Study

"Folklore" is a word that immediately conveys a set of stereotypes to most Americans, and it is necessary for this *Guide* to begin by contradicting several of them. If you already have a general interest in folklore (and most people seem to) the ideas set forth here should not destroy it. In fact, you will probably find that folklore is *more* interesting and varied than the popular books and articles you have read and the phonograph records or well-known singers you have heard would suggest. Despite widespread publicity and popular assumptions to the contrary, American folklore does not consist mainly of stories about Paul Bunyan, southern mountain ballads, protest songs, and fairy tales; nor is American folklore confined to rural regions or to past history. Instead, American folklore comprises a dazzling variety of types — including verbal, customary, and material aspects — and it continues to flourish in the present as it did in the past. It may even be safely said that anyone reading this *Guide* knows some folklore, has helped to circulate it, and could make a significant contribution to its study by collecting folklore. Such, at least, is the hope of the sponsors of this volume whose goal it is to stimulate the statewide collection, preservation, and study of the existing folklore of the State of Utah.

Nauvoo style or "I" house at Fountain Green,
Utah. Brickwork around windows and corners is
called "Dutch cross-bonding."   Photographed by Richard V. Francaviglia

When the word was coined by an English gentleman-scholar in 1846, "folklore" meant the "lore of the common folk," that is the archaic knowledge, customs, beliefs, sayings, stories, and songs of the rural commoners, or peasants. Gradually, as the study of folklore developed in Europe and the New World, it became apparent that the totality of any people's folk heritage extended far beyond what might reasonably be termed "lore" and that people of all classes and backgrounds shared some of these traditions in the present as well as the past. With the dimensions usually given the term by modern scholarship, "folklore" is taken to include *all* of the elements of a literate culture that are transmitted by word of mouth or by simple demonstration apart from books, schools, churches, or other commercial or institutionalized means. These folk elements may be purely verbal types (dialect, proverbs, riddles, rhymes, etc.), partly verbal types (superstitions, customs, festivals, games, etc.), or non-verbal types (gestures, music, architecture, arts, handicrafts, costumes, foods, etc.). In another organization (reflected in this *Guide*), the three general categories of folklore have been termed *folksay* (short verbal expressions), *folk literature* (longer narrative or poetic texts), and *folklife* (customary and material traditions).

The essence of all genuine folklore lies in (1) oral or customary transmission, (2) the creation of varying forms, and (3) possession by a "folk group." That is to say, authentic folklore is passed on by word of mouth or example in traditional forms that are constantly shifting and changing within some group of people who share one or more common traits, such as occupation, age, ethnic background, religion, or place of residence. Thus, a current joke circulating orally among computer programmers in variant forms is a piece of folklore, but a Paul Bunyan story (circulated in print, unvarying, and never actually part of lumberjack tradition) is not. As a consequence of oral transmission, much folklore is anonymous and the formal structure of folklore (whether verbal or not) tends to become relatively stereotyped: no one knows who made up most folktales or folk jokes, and they often begin with a stereotyped phrase like "Once upon a time . . ." or "There was this guy who. . . ." The changes that occur in folk transmission are usually unselfconscious, often accidental, and always within the prevailing traditional bounds recognized by the group. In contrast, fake folklore ("fakelore"), like Paul Bunyan stories, often has known authors and may be elaborately retold in literary or pseudo-folk style by each new editor. There is a world of difference between the actual sayings, songs, and stories of American loggers and the sentimentalized claptrap foisted upon them by writers of the Paul Bunyan books.

We cannot undertake here a full discussion of all the problems and questions raised by this modern scholarly conception of folklore versus the older, more popular and romantic one. (The further readings suggested at the end of this *Guide* will lead the interested reader into folklore scholarship.) The basic questions for a potential amateur collector of Utah folklore are probably these: "What is the purpose and importance of folklore study?" and "What might I do to help?"

Folklore is worth studying partly for the same reason that Everest was worth climbing or the moon is worth exploring — simply because it is there. Man has a natural and proper interest in himself and the world he lives in, and folklore, as an inescapable part of culture, demands to be interpreted and understood in terms of the rest of culture. If for no other reason than this there would be folklorists (students of folklore) to collect, archive (i.e., classify, file, and preserve), and analyze folklore; but there are further justifications of more importance.

Folklore by its very nature is underground, unofficial, uninhibited — in short, free and democratic. There are no effective restraints on what people may in some circumstances sing, say, tell, show, or teach to one another, and whenever these things become even slightly structured (as a proverb or a joke or a holiday custom, for instance) they may become part of folklore. Folk traditions, whether ancient or recent, have a tendency to preserve attitudes, beliefs, and sometimes even facts that are uniquely revealing of the people and cultures among whom the traditions circulate. Folklore study, then, is essential if we are to have a complete picture of man and his works in all their various shapes. This is true whether we study folklore in and for itself or, as is often done, in relation to other fields of investigation.

History, for example, should ideally be more than a dry recital of names, dates, statistics, treaties, and the like. We should not ignore the anecdotal, the rumored, the *human* side of history — what one American historian called "grass roots history." Seldom, of course, will folk traditions preserve a purely factual view of the past, but documents and research generally give us that side anyway. What folk traditions can contribute lies in the area of the spirit or "feeling" of a period. How much less colorful Utah history would be, for instance, without the legendary account of Brigham Young's first words upon seeing the Salt Lake Valley, "This is the place!" A whole superstructure of regional pride and pioneer-ancestor tradition has been based on that speech, and yet it cannot be precisely validated from historical sources. Nor can Jim Bridger's offer be documented of one thousand dollars for the first bushel (some say first *ear*) of corn grown in the valley; nor can Ebenezer

5

Bryce's alleged comment on the magnificent canyon that bears his name ("It's a hell of a place to lose a cow in!"). These speeches are part of the Utah folk heritage nonetheless, and an important, though perhaps unpretentious, part. They report how people imagine history ought to have been, even if not how it actually was. They, therefore, tell us something of how people perceive their heritage.

The common response of the early settlers to the harsh Rocky Mountain and Great Basin geography is another subject that facts alone can never recreate. Records of crop failures, facts about abandoned homesteads and townsites, reports of lost pioneering parties, and the like tell part of the story, but the audacious tall tales of the frontier and the songs, legends, and sayings about hard living in the drylands West tell more. The songs and brags of the cowboys; the stories about sheepherders, Chinamen, and Cornish miners; the accounts of lost mines, dream mines, and fabulous strikes; the oral sagas of confronting the Indians, founding new communities, and laying railroad lines all belong in the complete folk history of Utah.

Besides its documentary value in illuminating the human aspects of history, much folklore has considerable aesthetic appeal as well and ought to be preserved simply as a reminder of the artistic heights the human spirit is capable of sustaining on its own, even in an age of mass production, often tasteless popular arts, and constant commercial bombardment of all the senses. For instance, many of the folksongs of the United States — both imported and native products — have a charm and beauty of lyric and melody never duplicated either in the formal styles of art music or the faddish sounds of popular songs. The colors and traditional designs of a homemade quilt cannot be matched by an electric blanket. The clean functional lines of a pioneer stone house, combined with the textural appeal of the material and the heating efficiency of the construction, can put many a suburban split-level or "ranch style" home to shame. There is an appeal that the old clothespin doll or spool tank has in children's play that Barbie dolls and plastic racing cars fail to achieve. We are not suggesting that folk texts and artifacts should be collected so that they may be resurrected to displace modern inventions; folklore research, in the best sense, is not sentimental or antiquarian in purpose. But we should come to appreciate, through our studies of folklore, what the precious traditional heritage of our culture really *is*, what it *means*, and how it continues to shape our sensibilities.

With our emphasis on past folklore — that which is most quickly dying out and most needs to be preserved — we should not lose sight of the importance of collecting modern folklore, both the surviving vital part of older lore and the newly-created folk responses to contemporary life. After all, our own time eventually becomes part of the past, and we owe it to future generations to leave a record not only of formal, scientific, and academic accomplishments but also of human and common things. Besides, the study of presently living folklore is a key to understanding our own times, problems, and possibly some solutions to problems. Such current American concerns as racial relations, technology, environmental deterioration, and hope for peace are reflected in the folklore of the present. The folk games and rhymes of children, for instance, represent one of the great reservoirs of traditional response to the ongoing culture and its concerns, but very few folklorists in this country have specialized in their study. To cite one small example (and many more will follow), consider how one aspect of the widely-discussed "generation gap" and one prevailing modern social problem is reflected in the following song (a parody of the traditional round "Frère Jacques") which was collected last year from a ten-year-old boy in Salt Lake City:

Marijuana, marijuana,
LSD, LSD,
Scientists make it, teachers take it,
Why can't we, why can't we?

The thorough study and analysis of folklore involves many challenging theoretical matters and a host of specialists' talents ranging from those of the field worker, archivist, and indexer to linguists, ethnomusicologists, and cultural geographers. Again, the reader who wishes to penetrate further into this area is referred to the reading list appended to this *Guide*. But even the amateur folklorist with only minimal time to spare for his hobby can make a contribution to the study of Utah folklore by doing the task that is most basic and often the most *fun* as well — collecting. Since most folklore research in some way uses the technique of comparison, the bedrock basis of good scholarship in folklore is the careful collection of authentic folk texts and artifacts. This is where the previous study of Utah folklore is most lacking and where readers of this *Guide* may do much immediate good for the cause. This volume is intended to show you what to collect, how to collect, and where to deposit your material. Hopefully, this is the first step in a coordinated effort to fully document the existing folklore of Utah and make it available for study.

Notice should be taken here of past collections of Utah folklore, because some excellent efforts have been made, and a few good publications are already available covering special topics. For instance, Professor Austin E. Fife and Alta Fife of Utah State University have avidly collected for years the folklore of Utah Mormons and the general folklife of the western states; two of their numerous publications, major efforts that have won high praise from colleagues elsewhere, are *Saints of Sage and Saddle* (1956) and *Forms Upon the Frontier* (1969). Professor Emeritus Lester A. Hubbard of the University of Utah in his *Ballads and Songs of Utah* (1961) put into print only a portion of his voluminous collection of folksongs from Utah, and Professor Thomas E. Cheney of Brigham Young University rendered a similar service in his book *Mormon Songs from the Rocky Mountains* (1968). Other Utahns with important folklore publications to their names include Juanita Brooks of St. George, Olive Woolley Burt of Salt Lake City, and Hector Lee (now a California educator). These writers and others will be mentioned later, and their works are listed in the Bibliography. Besides the printed studies, some fairly comprehensive archival collections exist, both in the possession of instructors of folklore courses at universities in Utah and other states and in such depositories as the Utah State Historical Society and the now-defunct Utah Humanities Research Foundation.

The limitation of these previous efforts is that they stemmed from special projects and interests and they failed to constitute a complete coverage of all kinds of folklore from throughout the state. To accomplish this, a wider net of collectors is needed to be working under some kind of centralized advice and counsel, and here is where this *Guide* and its readers enter in.

We have not described in this volume all of the possible kinds of folklore to be found in Utah, but a range of typical types; we have not outlined here the most complete field documentation that a professional folklorist might produce, but a procedure detailed enough to supply adequate facts for worthwhile analysis. Our hope is that the examples and directions for collecting contained herein are simple, clear, and interesting enough so that every reader of the *Guide* — young or old, highly educated or not — will feel inspired to contribute something to the project. We ask that all materials be sent to the Utah Heritage Foundation and marked for permanent deposit in the folklore archive of either the University of Utah, Utah State University, or Brigham Young University.

To make this presentation as realistic as possible, the examples quoted throughout are taken verbatim from actual materials collected in the last four or five years by students in folklore classes at the University of Utah. The texts are deposited in the University of Utah Folklore Archive — a file of student term projects — and in most cases the examples are documented in this *Guide* only with the place and date they were recorded. Scattered examples with fuller documentation are included to show you exactly how a field text should look when written down for archiving.

Certainly many of these items are known throughout the state, as well as outside, but records at present are too incomplete to specify the distribution. There is clearly a geographical bias represented here for the Salt Lake Valley and Wasatch Front cities, the region from which many U of U students come. But for the sake of examples to study, the University Archive and undergraduate folklore classes already reveal a surprising range and variety of existing folklore materials. Learning how much more may exist depends now upon you, the reader. If, as you study the rest of this *Guide*, you find that you know similar examples or wish to do collecting of your own, we ask you, as a beginning, to fill out the Collector Data Sheet and the Questionnaire on Utah Birthday Customs at the end of this volume and mail them to the Utah Heritage Foundation, 603 E. South Temple, Salt Lake City, Utah 84102. If local groups are interested in organizing larger or more specialized collecting projects, the sponsors of this volume stand ready to advise and assist them. Bear in mind that the questions for field work at the end of each chapter are only suggestive, and feel free to use your own imagination in thinking up new categories for the folklore you find. You should designate where you want any material you submit put on permanent deposit, whether the University of Utah, Utah State University, or Brigham Young University.

Folk toy

My Father
Salt Lake City
November 23, 1969

When I was small, my father used to make toy tractors for me out of empty spools of thread. First he'd cut deep notches into the edge of the spool. Then he'd take a long rubber band and push it through the hole in the middle of the spool and stick a small piece of a match stick through one end of the elastic. He'd take a small round piece of soap, put a hole in the middle of it, and run the other end of the elastic through it so that the soap laid against the end of the spool. A large match stick was put through the end loop of the elastic next to the soap and he'd turn the match stick which twisted the elastic until it was tight. Then he'd set it on the floor and as the elastic unwound, the spool would crawl along the floor. It usually worked better on a rug.

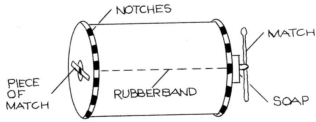

Linda Messerly

2

Suggestions
for Collecting Folklore

The first rule of successful collecting of folklore is to call it something else. Americans automatically associate the word "folklore" with groups — hillbillies, or lumberjacks, or pioneers perhaps — anyone but themselves. Most modern people will stoutly maintain that they wouldn't know any "folklore" personally, but "my late granddad" or "those lumberjacks," well! There are several ways to circumvent this tendency. One is to collect "on the fly," simply listening for and watching for examples of folklore in the course of daily life and recording them when they occur; this is an easy and natural method, but sometimes produces a very low, slow yield. Another good device is to ask people for generalized kinds of material — old-time songs, old family sayings or stories, old wives' tales, favorite jokes, jump rope rhymes, or hiccup cures. An almost surefire method is to relate folklore of your own and then wait for your listeners to top you, joke-for-joke, riddle-for-riddle, recipe-for-recipe.

The beginning collector should probably begin with himself, move on next to the rest of his family, and only later enter the "field," that is, into contact with people outside his normal round of acquaintances. Simply writing down *all* the folklore one individual knows, then that of his immediate family, and finally that of

An entry in a folklore archive.
A simple description and a sketch
are sufficient for a useful entry.

his neighborhood would be a long process, but extremely interesting and valuable to a folklorist and to oneself. Also, it would render much easier the eventual study of the folklore of that community or region.

When a professional folklorist conducts a field trip he usually has some specific question or hypothesis in mind which he intends to study. He generally does not collect all kinds of material at once, but concentrates his attention on limited and related matters. By the same token the amateur collector might want to "specialize" in one type of folklore (proverbs, children's games, fences and gates) or the lore of one specific group (hardrock miners, Basques, hunters). Once a collector becomes known locally as "the fellow who's collecting jokes" or the like, his quest becomes more fruitful.

The most important qualities of a usable text for folklorists are that it be verbatim from the lips of the "informant" (the human source) and be furnished with background data and context. Because people are sometimes spooked by the sudden appearance of a notebook or tape recorder, a good technique is only to look and listen at first, then ask permission to take some notes, and finally later try to write down or record all the words. Many folklorists carry a small notebook around strictly to keep tabs on potential informants and what they can narrate. Here one jots down the name and address, titles or types of material known, and questions to ask later. Once the collector has gained the trust of his informant, he might say, "I would like to take down all of your songs (or stories or whatever) because so many of these things are getting lost nowadays. But I can't remember it all as you told it. May I come back with my notebook (or tape recorder) and get it all down?" Then, as the collector revisits his informant, he can use the initial interview notes to jog his memory and organize the interview.

Again it must be emphasized — the *verbatim* text is desired. The exact words of the informant, complete with false starts, grammatical slips, and even pronunciation peculiarities, if possible. A tape recorder captures all of this (but *not* gestures, facial expressions, etc.); however, a recorder is not always available, and some informants dislike its use. Anyway, the tape must eventually be transcribed into written form if it is to be studied. Many folklorists, unless they are working with music, still prefer the old-fashioned notebook and pencil for collecting. The informant will have to pause now and then, and the collector will have to develop the ability to write at top speed, but it can be done. Do not abbreviate or summarize texts — get them *all* down.

The context and background data on a folk text should ideally be taken down at the same time as the lore. To whom is the item told? For what purpose? What is its apparent meaning, and what does the informant *say* it means? (Not necessarily the same thing.) What are the vital statistics on the informant: full name, address, age, background, sex, education, occupation, etc. Often a collector will begin to develop a fairly standard set of questions as he works in the field, something like this:

Where did you learn that?

When do you use it or tell it?

Do you believe it, or do others?

Do you know any other variations of that?

How does a collector know he is getting genuine folklore, and what should he do if the informant strays off the topic? Here the best rule is, "When in doubt, collect it!" If we only collected material that is already well documented as folklore, we would never discover any new kinds of folklore, and time and again folklorists have found that the apparently unique item from the field turns out upon study to be related to a wider tradition. If the informant seems to get off the point in an interview, of course he may be gently nudged back. But often the digressions and elaborations of a good informant cast just the sort of light on texts that folklorists treasure. If a tape recorder is being used, just keep it on — tape is relatively cheap and may be reused. If one is taking notes, at least jot down the subjects of the digressions.

Collecting with a tape recorder would seem to be the easiest thing in the world — just turn it on and let 'er rip. But a little bit of care and technique is needed to make this technical aid serve us well. First, one should always master his equipment *before* entering the field with it, learning how high to set the volume and where to place the mike for maximum performance. Generally it is best to set the tape in motion at a standard speed, place the mike solidly down, and leave it running thereafter without unnecessary fiddling with the controls. Keeping the rotating tape reels out of sight of the informant helps to relax him. The taped interview should always begin with some kind of introduction identifying the individuals to be heard, the place, and the date. The tape reel or leader tape should be clearly labeled with subject and tape speed, as should the reel box, and an index should be prepared showing what was recorded and in what order.

Most collectors, we expect, will not be using a tape recorder in the field, at least not at first. These collectors should prepare their material, neatly typed or handwritten, on one side of $8\frac{1}{2} \times 11$-inch paper or 3×5-inch index cards. Short items go on cards, long ones on sheets, with each item identified by type of folklore,

13

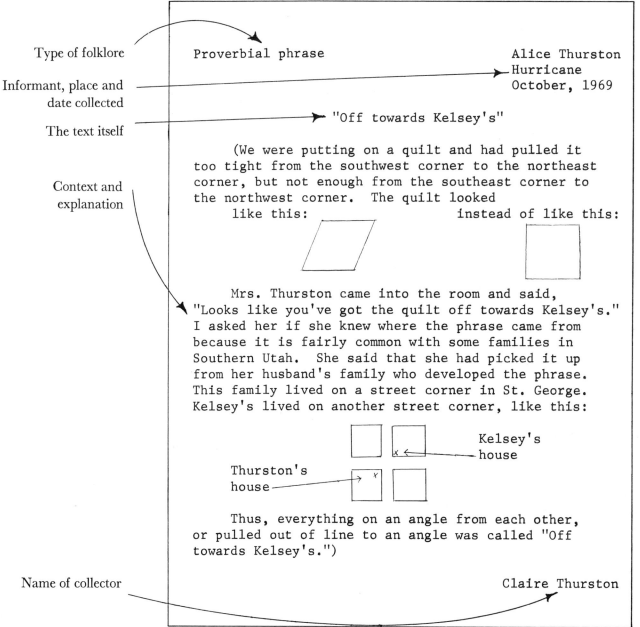

Type of folklore

Informant, place and
date collected

The text itself

Context and
explanation

Proverbial phrase

Alice Thurston
Hurricane
October, 1969

"Off towards Kelsey's"

(We were putting on a quilt and had pulled it
too tight from the southwest corner to the northeast
corner, but not enough from the southeast corner to
the northwest corner. The quilt looked
like this: instead of like this:

Mrs. Thurston came into the room and said,
"Looks like you've got the quilt off towards Kelsey's."
I asked her if she knew where the phrase came from
because it is fairly common with some families in
Southern Utah. She said that she had picked it up
from her husband's family who developed the phrase.
This family lived on a street corner in St. George.
Kelsey's lived on another street corner, like this:

Kelsey's
house

Thurston's
house

Thus, everything on an angle from each other,
or pulled out of line to an angle was called "Off
towards Kelsey's.")

Name of collector

Claire Thurston

14

informant, place and date collected, and name of collector. A proverbial phrase, exactly as collected by a student from her mother, with all the necessary information given in the proper places, is illustrated, as is a similar but short item which would go on a 3×5 card.

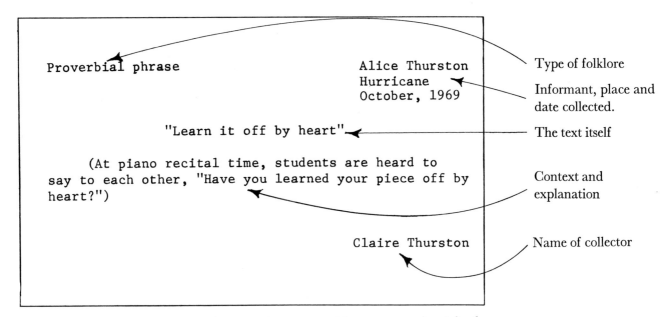

Each informant should be identified by name, address, age, national background, and education — as a minimum — but when a collector interviews several informants and is sending in material from each one, it is convenient to make an alphabetized list of informants' names with the background data for each one summarized. Then users of the material will have the means for looking up added information about sources only identified by name, place, and date with the texts. Any informant who is outstanding, either for quantity or quality of texts, ought to be written up in more detail, stressing his personality, his use of folklore, his style, and the relation of his folk material to his life. By way of example, here is a good sketch of the informant for the last two quoted items:

> *Mrs. Alice Woodbury Thurston was born in La Verkin, Utah, on July 18, 1906. She attended school there until her family moved to Hurricane, Utah, about one mile away, about seven years later. She remembers milking cows each night after her older brothers left home, and of taking over their chores of pitching hay and dry farm-*

15

ing. Much of her early life was spent in practicing the piano (to get out of doing the dishes), playing ball in the lane next to her home, going to school, swimming in the canal and foot-racing. It is one of her primary recollections that she could beat any boy in town at running.

When Mrs. Thurston was in high school she eloped to Parowan with a school teacher, Paul Thurston. Shortly after she moved to Enterprise where her husband was scheduled to teach. During his career as a teacher they moved many times in the southern Utah area. One summer they lived in a tent in Springdale while her husband worked as a naturalist in Zion National Park. That summer they put on an operetta in the natural amphitheatre in the park. The operetta was called "Pioneer Papoose." Mrs. Thurston played the piano which had been hauled there especially for the purpose and held her youngest daughter Thais on her lap while she played. At that time, she had three children.

Her husband decided to go back to school, this time to the University of Utah, so Mrs. Thurston went along and studied piano under Charley Shepard at the McCune School of Music. She remembers that if you made the same mistake twice, he would knock your fingers from the keyboard.

After finishing his bachelor's degree at the University, her husband decided to go to school at the University of Chicago. While he was gone Mrs. Thurston went to Hurricane and rented the apartment her parents had built in their house. To pay her rent she taught piano lessons. When her husband graduated with an M. S. from the University of Chicago she went back to see him graduate. Mr. Thurston was engaged in work on his PhD when their youngest daughter Tamara became ill of cancer, so he accepted a position as Superintendent of Schools at Overton, Nevada, and the family moved there. Shortly after the birth of another daughter, Emma Louise, Tamara died. Not long after that, Mrs. Thurston had a heat stroke and her husband decided to return to Hurricane and take up ranching. Mrs. Thurston is still living in Hurricane and teaches piano and organ lessons. She also writes music and poetry. She believes in saving everything, "because you never know when it will be useful."

Claire Thurston
Fall, 1969

So far we have assumed that the collector is only taking down *texts*, the actual words of verbal folklore, along with their contexts. But what about the techniques for collecting customary or material folk traditions, what we call "folklife" data? Here the guidelines would be to describe it, measure it, and if possible illustrate it. The description, art work, or photography of folklife data need not be elaborate or highly skilled, just so it is clear. In the collection of "Off towards Kelsey's" already illustrated, for example, the sketches are roughly made, but the full and logical description makes the saying and its use perfectly understandable. Often it is possible to have the informant himself describe how an artifact is made or how a game is played or a dance done, but this should not be left to stand alone; generally the collector may clarify these "folk" explanations with observations or pictures of his own. In many instances, when collecting "on the fly," the informant cannot be fully identified or quoted; an example of how this sort of situation may be taken down appears in this illustration.

```
Superstition                          Middle-aged man
                                      Bountiful
                                      March, 1969


     I work in a milk depot in Bountiful.  One night a
customer came in and bought some yogurt.  He told me
that in the winter he often got cold sores on his
mouth.  He said that if you eat two servings of yogurt
each day it will cure cold sores, and if you keep
eating it each day it will keep them from coming back.


                                      Linda Messerly
```

When collecting pictures of buildings or objects it is highly important to keep close track of what you photograph in what order and where. Nothing is harder to sort out than a mixed batch of slides or negatives from a long field trip during which numerous similar items were discovered. After a while all the hay derricks and granaries begin to look alike, at least in the pictures. This is not the place to go into details on camera techniques except to emphasize that the folk object is the only important subject, and everything else should be subordinate to that. The pictures

17

in this volume demonstrate these points: get up close, focus carefully, look for simple uncluttered backgrounds, and try to have something in the picture to suggest the size or scale of the item being photographed.

Cameras, tape recorders, and other gadgets help to facilitate folklore collecting, but time after time you will find that pencil and paper used to write a clear description and make a simple sketch will do the job adequately.

3

Some Folk Groups of Utah

For convenience, the rest of this *Guide* is organized around types of folk traditions, although in actual experience one does not find all of the proverbs and riddles and quilts and rail fences neatly sorted out in separate places. More likely, one might pass by a rail fence on his way to a quilting bee where an occasional proverb or riddle is spoken during breaks in a television program. Quite commonly, collectors are concerned more with the various traditions of a folk group rather than with any one type of lore. Studying a folk group thoroughly involves looking into some aspects of the group's life beyond the strictly folk ones.

To begin with, what *is* a folk group? As already stated, we may use the term for any group that shares some common trait out of which spring some shared traditions; in other words, a folk group is any group that has some distinctive folklore. As roundabout as this definition may sound, it works very well in practice. Thus, when collecting folklore, one may begin by alerting himself for the in-group traditions of lingo and lore before establishing precisely what the folk group is that circulates these traditions.

Folk groups are in some way isolated from the general population that surrounds them, but not necessarily isolated by living in the remote hills many miles

Copper mining crew near St. George,
1898 or 1899   Courtesy Utah Mining Association

from neighbors and conveniences. Isolation may be geographical only in that a distinctive topography surrounds them (as the Great Basin or Utah's "Dixie"); it might be cultural, perhaps in terms of church membership (i.e., Latter-day Saints, Catholic, or Unitarian); or it might be produced by some temporary status (such as age or military service). It is clear, then, that most people participate in several different folk groups at one time and in different groups at various stages of life. Of course, not every possible human grouping will have distinctive folklore, but a great number of groups do have it; for instance, there is folklore in Utah of, by, and about the geographic region, religious groups, children, and military servicemen.

A person shares the traditions of his folk group (or groups) unconsciously and casually. He enters as an outsider, newcomer, greenhorn, or the like (as when beginning a new job or moving to a new home), but soon he acquires a sense of the group's mystique and begins to use its special language and take part in its expected customs and rituals. Initiations into groups may be relatively formal, such as in college fraternal organizations or lodges, or it may consist of informal hazing, or just gradual acceptance by new friends and neighbors. Without really being aware of the transitions they make, people move easily from the proper behavior for such folk groups as occupational or peer groups to that of family and social life. For example, the returned serviceman may have to explain, rephrase, or censor his "army" language when he is home on leave, and the teenager needs two different vocabularies to talk with his contemporaries and with his grandparents. In order to record the folklore of a group thoroughly, the collector (whether he belongs to the group or not) must train himself to "tune in" on the aspects of group interaction that are traditionally structured and orally transmitted. For example, the official theology and ritual of a religious group are not folklore, but terms like "Jack Mormon," "Hardshell Baptist," and "Mackerel Snapper" are.

To guide Utah folklore collectors in the field, let us review briefly some of the prominent folk groups of this state. In outline, we might say that they consist primarily of Indians, Mormons, immigrants, and occupational groups.

We shall not be concerned much here with the Indians of Utah, for the study of their cultures belongs to the special province of the anthropologist who is trained in the techniques of linguistic, cultural, physical, and ethnohistorical analysis. Besides, in such groups lacking a written native language it is impossible to distinguish aspects of culture as "folk" or "non-folk"; the whole culture is traditional. However, it would be a mistake not to bear the Indians in mind when collecting Utah folklore, for the Indian theme is prominent in white folklore, and problems of Indian-white relations are expressed in a body of intergroup lore that the anthropologists seldom notice.

The Mormons, of course, are the largest and best-known group in Utah, and consequently the group most often collected from in the past. Folklore among Utah Mormons is rich and distinctive, paralleling as it does the whole saga of development of the Church of Jesus Christ of Latter-day Saints from founding and early persecution to westward migration, settlement, and eventual flourishing. The songs and legends of settling Utah, the anecdotes about prominent churchmen, the pioneer folkways, the lore of faith and folly, and miracles and missionaries of Mormondom have all become part of the heritage and will be touched on in the examples of this survey.

Immigrant groups in Utah may be those heavily converted to Mormonism, such as Scandinavians, Dutch, English, German, and Austrian, or they may have come here principally for other than religious reasons, as did many Italians, Greeks, Mexicans, and Japanese. Whether Mormon or not, a person's degree of sharing in his immigrant group lore may vary depending upon how many generations ago his family emigrated, how clannish the settlement patterns were, and how actively the group maintained Old World customs. Furthermore, a member of such a group may possess much or little of his ethnic traditional heritage along with group lore of his occupation, region, or other cultural contacts as well. An ethnic group of particular interest to folklorists in Utah and surrounding states is that of the Basques. Often hired as sheepherders, they are proud of their unique culture and careful to keep in contact with their homeland's traditions.

The occupational groups of Utah overlap with the regional, religious, and ethnic groups because, obviously, workers are also Mormons, non-Mormons, converts, immigrants, natives, etc. Therefore, we find situations like these: the hard-rock miners of Park City, the coal miners of Carbon county, and the copper miners of Bingham Canyon all have developed characteristic mining folklore of their trades and regions, but also often have some ethnic traditions of the Irish, Italian, Greek, or other backgrounds, and in general they are non-Mormons. Ranchers, farmers, and orchardists of Utah, on the other hand, are likely to be Mormons and also of other national stock than the miners. The possibilities of occupational folk traditions in Utah have barely been touched so far, and one can only list some other groups that are obvious—railroad workers, tour guides, heavy construction workers, smelter and factory laborers, race car drivers, musicians, and so forth. Perhaps we

23

should also include groups that are organized periodically for a limited time, such as religious retreats, children's summer camps, army reserve and national guard active duty, and the like.

All the examples of folklore in this *Guide* come from some group or other, perhaps only a family, but even the family traditions (like "Off towards Kelsey's") may be more widely circulated. We can take a few examples of a more distinct group's lore by way of demonstrating what can be collected.

Miners, of whatever minerals, all over the state follow the practice of hazing new men and playing practical jokes on each other to test and maintain group spirit. The natural butt of many jokes was the new man from abroad:

> *There were lots of miners that came over from the old country after some of their relatives come here. Most of them couldn't speak English, so they had quite a time. One time one of them turned up with a tag around his neck saying "Deliver to Con O'Neil." Con was the mine foreman at the Silver King for years, and was one of the best known of the Irish characters. (Park City, 1967)*

Men in the Park City mines put their town clothes in a basket before going to work in their mine clothes; the basket was hauled up to the ceiling of the change room on a chain and then padlocked in place. If a man forgot to lock his chain, he was in trouble:

> *Sometimes somebody forgets to lock up their clothes, or has brought them down and gone under the shower. He's just asking for it, and somebody soon chews beef with his clothes. One time a guy did this, but good! He got an iron bar, put it through the arms of a coat, bent it around, and welded it together! (Park City, 1967)*

Another favorite trick was to take a lunch bucket apart and nail the bottom to the bench so that when it was picked up it would come apart. Or a man might break a tamping stick in half, wrap it to look like a stick of dynamite, set a fuse in it, light it, and throw it into the "dog house" where others were sitting around talking or playing cards.

Reports from the Bingham mines include the age-old pranks of sending men for "slag pumps," "rail stretchers," and "sky hooks." Here is a prank a folklore student himself suffered recently during summer employment there:

> *When a person begins to work on a track gang at the Kennecott Copper Corporation Bingham Mine he must learn to drive*

railroad spikes. When he feels he is getting pretty good at it, one of the older members of the gang will make this proposition: "If you can drive that spike in thirty swings, I'll buy you a malt. If you can't you buy the gang malts." Of course the new man knows he can drive a spike in less than thirty swings, so he agrees. But twenty swings is not thirty, so he loses. (Salt Lake City, 1967)

As a man learns the job, passes the tests, and achieves the respect of his co-workers, he begins to play pranks of his own, and he may acquire a nickname. In the Eureka mining area of Utah, for instance, many nicknames of miners have been recorded, including "Muck Pile Johnny" for a good shoveler, "Mushmouth Garcia" for a Mexican with some teeth missing who was hard to understand, and "Oily Jack" for a longtime hoistman in the mine.

Part Two

Folk Traditions of Utah

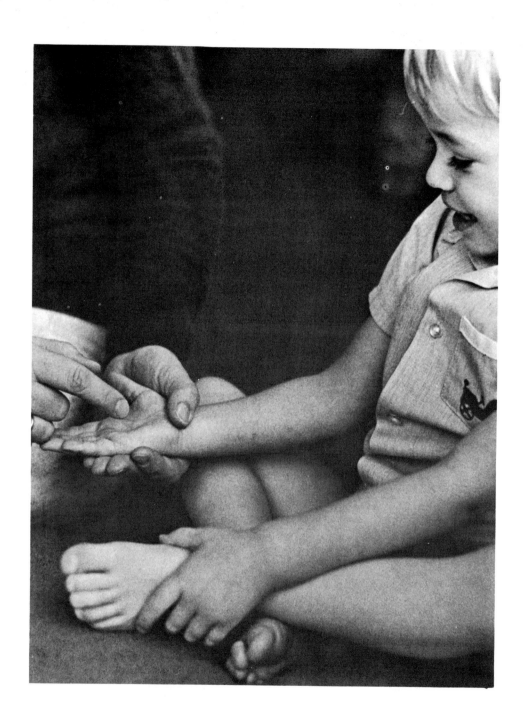

4

Folksay

The short verbal folk expressions that do not constitute a complete story or point of view about something have been termed "folksay"; that is, things people say in traditional words, phrases, or rhymes. Such sayings do not occur in a vacuum, of course, but rather they are usually part of a longer folk type (such as tale or song), or they spring to mind as conventional responses to particular situations or needs. No matter what type of folklore the collector is seeking he may hear instances of folksay, and it is a good idea to take note of these when the chances happen. One or two dialect terms or riddles may not seem important at the time, but if every reader sent in that much we would have a substantial harvest. The typical kinds of folksay are dialect and naming, proverbs, riddles, and rhymes.

Dialect and Naming

Dialect (sometimes called "folk speech"), in the sense that we use the term here, refers to non-standard modes of speech characteristic of a regional or other folk groups. This may involve pronunciation, grammar, or word choice (vocabulary, including traditional naming). Collecting the distinctive traditional speech

Finger-counting rhymes
used to amuse a child

Photographed by Douglas Hill and William A. Wilson

patterns of a group is often one of the best ways of getting introduced to that group and learning its special language to facilitate further collecting.

In Utah the best known feature of local pronunciation is the alteration of the vowel sounds "a" and "o" before the consonant "r." There are many anecdotes about the pronunciation of place names ("Amarican Fark") and local terms ("Farth Ward"), but the idea that there is a *regular* reversal of "a" and "o" in Utah seems to be a myth. That is, not every speaker reverses all of the sounds, though some may actually say things like "He was barn in a born," or "Porden me, ore you taking your core to the porty in the pork?" Collectors should listen for particular catch phrases or sentences like these that people use to illustrate "Utah pronunciation." Another matter to note is the local way of pronouncing place names, such as Weber, Heber, Tooele, Hurricane, Manti, Callao, etc.

Grammatical dialect variations are often collected simply by overhearing them in use. What we are after here, as folklorists, is not so much just the "bad" grammar common in everyday speech everywhere in the country ("ain't," "being as," "to be enthused," etc.) but the peculiar turns of speech characteristic of a region or occupation that deviate from casually spoken general American speech. If a collector thinks he hears an odd phrase, the best thing to do is write it down:

> *I overheard the cook in the Carlson Hall dormitory kitchen say to the girls working in the cafeteria serving line, "Here's ya some eggs." (Salt Lake City, 1969)*
>
> *"I told her there was no way I'd bowl this year." (This is a common expression for giving emphasis to a statement of impossibility.) (Salt Lake City, 1969)*

It is useful to add a note on variations for such usages that you may know yourself:

> *"Place backs" is what my cousins call out when they leave their chairs for some reason, and want to return to the same chair. If they do not call "place backs," then anyone else in the room may take their place. (This is similar to terms I used when I was young to secure my rights to something, like a piece of candy. We called this "dibs" or "dubs," or sometimes we said "I dubs it!")*
>
> *(Salt Lake City, 1969)*

The richest harvest of dialect data that a beginner in linguistic field work can gather is vocabulary. In fact, one of the major things to prepare for any folk group you study is a glossary of the special terms they use and their meanings. If possible, definitions should be in the informant's own words and examples or descriptions of the terms used in context should be secured.

Generally speaking, we "folk" are unaware of our special vocabulary. For example, Utahns of all persuasions become familiar with the limited meaning in use here for the term "Gentile" and the connotations of "Jack Mormon" or "Mormon tea" (hot water with cream and sugar added) without realizing that such terms are unknown or used differently elsewhere. A subgroup within the Mormon community may have its own vocabulary terms; missionaries speak of a "golden contact," or a "greenie" (new man in the field), and they are said to be "riding the trunks" or "sitting on their trunks" when they are ready to pack and come home. In a cultural climate that frowns on swearing, sham swear words and phrases or substitutes like "fudge," "flip," and "scrud" are heard. The phrases include "Summer ditch and dirty basket" and "Holy jumped-up cheese and rice." One student made this report:

> *A woman was buying a prescription, and when she opened her purse and found her money was at home she said "Oh, Holy Kodava!" When she left, I asked the druggist if he had ever heard the expression. He said he had, but it was "Gadova" not "Kodava."*
> *(Salt Lake City, 1969)*

Sometimes there may be no logical explanation for an unusual term, and the collector or informant may simply guess. Obviously, collecting something like this is a gamble, but we may never learn if it is folklore without putting it on record as a possibility.

Lists of terms should especially be collected from occupational groups, and these may be sent in either on separate 3×5-inch cards or in alphabetical order on sheets. To take a few scattered examples from Utah informants, theater people refer to complimentary tickets as "Annie Oakleys" or "twofers" (two tickets for the price of one, generally). Military servicemen refer to the "brown boots army" (old army) and "black boots army" (new); a haircut should be "white sidewalls" in the army, and cleaning up the barracks is a "GI party." Some meat cutters and wrappers will refer to packaged chicken parts as "his" or "hers," depending upon whether an extra breast or leg is added; beef tongues are "lickers" and kidneys are "pee strainers." Warehousemen may receive an "av-check" as a bonus if production is up to a set standard; filling orders at the optimum rate is "running an av." Hunters who have to tramp through rough country may say they are "brush busting" or "Tooley busting."

```
Dialect term                         Judy Law
                                     Roy
                                     October 15, 1969

    Taw:  My father uses this word to mean "Thank
you" when someone passes food to him at the dinner
table.

    (Judy said she thinks it is an English word
because both of her father's parents were British.)


                                     Marianne Faulkner
```

(The only even remote possibility to compare with the above in *The English Dialect Dictionary* of 1962 is "Taw" as an interjection in the sense of "silence!" or "hark!")

```
Dialect                              Robert J. Birkbeck
Occupational term                    Salt Lake City
(mining)                             (Raised in Park City)
                                     July 19, 1967

    Widowmaker:  This is the name given to the jack-
hammer because the man lies on it with his stomach to
hold it down and it shakes him to pieces.  A lot of
men were really killed that way.


                                     Eleanor H. Carlston
```

Here, without the definitions, is a partial list of mining names and terms collected from one Park City miner. An example quoted in full is also illustrated.

Dead man	Nipper
Dog house	Old man, the
Drill doctor	Ore picker
Gallows frame	Rope man
Honey dipper	Shift boss
Horse doctor or barn man	Skinner
Jigger boss	Station tender
Machine man	Stope boss
Motorman	Timberman
Mucker	Trammer

The slang and jargon of the present should be recorded as thoroughly as the outmoded terms of the past. Here are some examples from Salt Lake City student slanguage:

Backspace. *This term is used when someone makes a verbal mistake. It comes from the term in typing. (1966)*

Customized. *A crashed or wrecked person or thing. If a car has been in an accident, you can ironically say it was "customized." (1969)*

```
Dialect                          Kirk Jensen
Occupational term                Salt Lake City
(computers)                      November 17, 1969


    Gigo:  You know what that means?  G-i-g-o,
"Garbage in, garbage out."  That's what happens to
those computers, same as anything else.




                                 Ronald Howard
```

33

Cancer juice. Pre-sweetened juice drinks containing cyclamates.
(1969)

Longhairs. Hippies or other individuals with long hair; by asso-
ciation, dirty or repulsive people. (1969)

If you are making a conscious effort to collect dialect terms and folk naming, it is a good idea eventually to draw up a set of questions to ask people. These should take the form of a description of some thing or situation for which the informant supplies his own natural word. For instance, you could ask "What do you call a little bit more of something?" and the answer might be "smidgen," "tad," "touch," or "skosch." Or "What do you call crossing an intersection diagonally?" Variations include "kitty-corner," "J-walking," "catacorner," "cut-across," "criss-cross," and "cross-cutting." One good question has to do with the accepted answer to "Thank you"; although many Utahns will answer that they always say "You're welcome," what they often actually say is "You bet." As you begin to collect dialect, bear the following questions in mind too:

What sentences or anecdotes have you heard that illustrate supposed "Utah pronunciation?"

Can your informants describe or imitate a "Utah drawl"?

How do people pronounce the words "creek," "route," "coyote," and "peony." Do these or other words get pronounced in more than one way in Utah?

Can you compile a glossary of terms (with definitions) used in a particular hobby, occupation, job, or region?

Can you collect a whole sentence or paragraph using a high percentage of specialized terms?

Do you know any traditional names for or ways of calling certain animals?

Do you have any unusual family words, expressions, or sayings?

Have you ever had occasion to explain a typical Utah term to a tourist or other visitor? What was it, and how did you explain it?

Proverbs

Proverbs, strictly speaking, are traditional sentences expressing general truths or wisdom and often making use of rhyme, assonance, alliteration, and other poetic devices. But the term "proverb" is also stretched to include comparisons and metaphoric phrases as well. Thus, in common usage, a sentence such as "like attracts like" is a *true proverb*, the phrase "hotter than the hubs of Hell" is a *proverbial comparison*, and one like "going on a wild goose chase" is a *proverbial phrase*. A rarer variety of proverb is the *Wellerism* or quotation proverb: " 'A little goes a long way,' as the man said when he spit over the cliff."

True proverbs are usually arranged in archives or publications in alphabetical order according to the first noun, as are these examples from Utah:

> *When the* apple's *ripe it will fall.*
>
> *When* children *are little they step on your toes; when they're grown they step on your hearts.*
>
> *He who lays a good* egg *has the right to cackle.*
>
> *Save the* pennies; *the dollars will take care of themselves.*
>
> *Three can keep a* secret, *if two are dead.*
>
> *A* woman *convinced against her will is of the same opinion still.*
>
> *A poor* workman *complains about his tools.*

However, instead of recording merely a list of proverbs, the collector, as with all types of folklore, should take note of the context as well as the text. Notice how the informants' apparent meanings for related proverbs vary in the two examples illustrated.

Proverb
                                            Eugene W. Sloan
Salt Lake City
November 2, 1969

    The bishop of my church, addressing the congregation about how much they should donate to the budget said: "Let's not wait until the wheel squeaks before calling for the grease."

                                           Caron Madsen

Proverb

Sydney Johnson
Salt Lake City
November 19, 1969

   While talking to her brother, a friend of mine
said that he should study more to receive superior
grades. She said, "Remember, the greasy axle gets the
wheel." This refers to the fact that the proper type
of preparation produces favorable results. If the
axle weren't greased, the wheel would not be placed
upon it.

Marc Ordman

In the following instance what is regarded by the collector as a family saying
is a traditional proverb paraphrasing Biblical language (see Luke 14:5) with wide
circulation among Mormons to justify work on Sundays.

Proverb

Mary E. Tassainer
Salt Lake City
October 20, 1967

   Sometimes my dad had work to do on Sunday, and he
would work instead of going to church. The church
members would come by and comment about working on
Sunday. He always said the same thing: "I see it
this way; when a horse is stuck in the mud, pull him
out."

   (This has become a standard phrase in our family.)

Alice Kaye Tassainer

Proverbial comparisons may be arranged in a collection alphabetically by the quality that is being compared:

> better *than his bond*
>
> blacker *than the inside of a black cat*
>
> *so* crooked *he has to screw his socks on*
>   *(variant: so* tight *he screws his shoes on)*
>
> *all* dressed up *like a yard of pump water*
>
> hotter *than a fox in a forest fire*
>
> tighter *than Dick's hatband*

Again, however, context is preferred, as in this example:

> *My mother says this whenever she serves apple pie and cheese: "Apple pie without the cheese is like a kiss without the squeeze." Once when we didn't have any cheese to go with the pie she said, "Sorry to have to give the kiss without the squeeze."*
> *(Salt Lake City, 1969)*

An informant's comments or explanation for a proverb sometimes indicates how facts can be changed in oral transmission:

> *Her grandmother's phrase for "It isn't worth a cent" was "It ain't worth a Continental." She says a Continental was a silver piece from the Continent used during the early colonial period. After the Constitution, she says, the money was worthless. (The* Random House Dictionary *of 1967 says that a Continental was paper currency issued by the Continental Congress during the American Revolution. The saying itself is explained as "a small amount, advice that's not worth a Continental.") (Salt Lake City, 1969)*

Many modern proverbial expressions function as insults, retorts, wisecracks, and ironic commentaries. A bad driver in Utah has been described as "an accident looking for a place to happen." A female social event may be a "hen party." An annoying person is told, "Put an egg in your shoe and beat it!" A person leaving a job is told, "We won't miss you any more than the hole left when you stick your finger in a glass of water." Other commonly heard expressions are euphemistic references to sensitive subjects, like "Charley's dead" or "It's snowing down south" for a slip that is showing, the term "Granny" for the menstrual period, and "up a stump" for pregnancy.

Here are three further examples of sayings applied to specific situations:

"I'm doing the fine print in my contract." (This was the informant's reply upon being questioned about why she was washing dishes in the cafe where she works as a waitress.)

(Salt Lake City, 1969)

My professor in the University of Utah Biology Department would say, "If you kids don't study hard for this final, I'm afraid you've bought the ranch, *because it's a hard one." (1967)*

"We have pasteurized water; it runs through every pasture in town." (Common saying in Ferron, Utah, before they installed the water treatment plant.) (Orem, 1967)

In Utah, with its many citizens of immigrant backgrounds, one may collect foreign proverbs still in use, sometimes in the native language and also in translation. The following were translated and used just as English proverbs, though their informants recognized them as foreign. If possible the original language should be collected as well.

Two Hungarians, three opinions. (Hungarian proverb)

If you go to Seville you lose your seat. (Spanish saying used when one leaves his seat and comes back to find it taken by another.)

Monday comes before Sunday. (Swedish saying for "Your slip is showing.")

While collecting proverbs and proverbial expressions, these questions might be kept in mind:

If you concentrate on listening for proverbial expressions for a set time (perhaps one hour), how many and which ones do you hear? In what situations were they used?

Do you know any Wellerisms?

Do older people in your family or community have any favorite pieces of proverbial advice they like to use?

Do younger people know parodies of traditional proverbs?

Have you observed proverbs used in advertising, editorials, sermons, lectures, or other such contexts?

What proverbial responses do you have for special uses, such as referring to socially taboo topics, death, good or bad luck, children's misbeavior, and so forth?

What proverbs do you feel are peculiarly Mormon?

Riddles

Various traditional questions, verbal puzzles, problems, and catches are lumped together under the general head of "riddles." A few are *true riddles* — fairly complex formal descriptions that refer to an unexpected answer to resolve the illogic of the question. True riddles in American tradition are often from Old World folklore, as the subjects and style of the first two examples below suggest, but they may be, like the next two, somewhat localized.

Flower of England,
Fruit of Spain,
Met together in a shower of rain.
Put in a cloth,
Tied with a string,
If you'll tell me this riddle,
I'll give you a ring.

Answer: a plum pudding.
(Salt Lake City, 1968)

Riddle   Areta Ruth Rigby
                                          Centerville
                                          October 15, 1967

          Come a riddle
          Come a raddle
          Come a rote tote tote.
          A wee, wee man
          With a red, red coat,
          A staff in his hand
          And a stone in his throat.

          What is it?
          (Answer: A cherry.)

                                      William M. Sill

A riddle, a rhyme
I suppose.
A hundred eyes,
But never a nose.

Answer: a potato
(Farmington, 1967)

Upon a hill
There stands a red bull;
He eats and he eats,
And he never gets full.
What is it?

Answer: a threshing machine
(Centerville, 1967)

Puzzling questions that defy the logic of true riddles and involve tricks or special wit for solution are called *riddling questions*:

Why did they bury the light-headed Irishman on the side of the hill? Answer: because he was dead. (Salt Lake City, 1969)

What goes up when rain comes down? Answer: an umbrella.
(Salt Lake City, 1967)

Such riddling questions as involve puns are *conundrums*:

```
Conundrum                              Monte Sill
                                       Farmington
                                       September 30, 1967

    How many apples were eaten in the Garden of Eden?

    Answer:  Eleven.  Adam ate (eight), Eve too
(two), and Satan won (one).



                                       William M. Sill
```

What is bought by the yard and worn by the foot? Answer: a carpet. (Salt Lake City, 1967)

What do you call a cow that can't give milk? Answer: an udder failure. (Salt Lake City, 1968)

Do you know why the mouse got pregnant at Albertsons? Answer: Because she didn't know there was a Safeway.

(Salt Lake City, 1968)

In the past, adults sometimes used riddles, especially true riddles, as mental tests and exercises for children. Some parents or grandparents would reward a child for those he could guess correctly. Children among themselves tend rather to use riddles as jokes, just telling them and their answers rapidly to each other and not waiting for any serious guessing. Another device popular with children is the *catch question* in which the listener is victimized:

Hinch me and pinch me
Went out for a ride.
Hinch me fell out,
So who was left?
 Listener says "pinch me" and the riddler does.
 (Salt Lake City, 1969)

What's the first sign of insanity?
 Answer: hair on your knuckles.
What's the second sign?
 Answer: looking for it.
 (Salt Lake City, 1969)

Recently a series of absurd *riddle-jokes* has been circulating among children and adolescents:

What's purple and conquered the world?
  Answer: Alexander the Grape.
What's purple and has twenty-seven wives?
  Answer: Brigham Plum.
  (both Salt Lake City, 1968)

What do you get when you cross an elephant with a jar of peanut butter? Answer: Either an elephant that sticks to the roof of your mouth or a jar of peanut butter that never forgets.

(Salt Lake City, 1967)

Comparable to riddles, which are guessing problems, are *tongue-twisters* which are pronunciation problems.

41

Tongue-twister

Mark Eatough
Salt Lake City
(Has lived in
Mercur, Bingham,
Park City, and
Eureka.)
Fall, 1969

The grasshoppers come e't off all of Eatough's wheat off.

(Evidently the early settlers had fun with the name "Eatough" as the kids did when I was growing up. Mark Eatough is my father. The grasshoppers referred to are the Mormon crickets, and the crickets <u>had</u> devoured my forefather's wheat. This tongue-twister saying was used by way of greeting the early Eatoughs. It is now repeated when we tell funny stories connected with the name.)

Nancy Johnston

> *Around the rugged rock the ragged rascal ran.*
>
> *A skunk sat on a stump. The skunk thunk the stump stunk, and the stump thunk the skunk stunk.*
>
> *Pretty party Polly painted purple pearls partly for pretty pining princesses, partly portly prim princes.*
>
> *Wir Wiener Waschweiber würden weisse Wäsche waschen wenn wir wüssten wo warmes Wasser Wäre. (A German tongue-twister collected in Salt Lake City in 1968)*

Mnemonic devices are a special class of tricky sentences that may be included here. These use their initial letters as memory aids for factual information. Among the areas they treat are music, geography, spelling, and science.

> *A rat in the house might eat the ice cream.*
> *A rich Irishman thought he might eat Tom's ice cream.*
> > *(Two devices for spelling "arithmetic.")*
> *Mark's very extravagant mother just sent us nine parakeets.*
> *Many very energetic monkeys jumped sidewise under nut plants.*
> > *(Two devices for the planets in their space order from the sun.)*
> *Neither financier seized either weird species of leisure.*
> > *(A sentence containing some of the exceptions to the " 'i' before 'e' " spelling rule.)*

Collectors of riddles of any variety should be alert to take notice of the riddles themselves, their meanings and functions, and the situations in which they are transmitted. Local references in riddling texts are especially interesting, but they should be fully explained when they are sent in. These questions may guide you in the field:

What riddles, conundrums, catch questions, or riddle-jokes do you know? Write them all down, no matter how common, just as a measure of riddle popularity.

How are riddles told in your community or family? Are they used as a guessing game, as a "concert," a means to test children, etc.?

Do you know anyone who has a notebook or scrapbook of riddles?

Have you ever heard of rewarding children with coins or treats for guessing riddles correctly?

What mnemonic devices do you know for spelling, music, science, or other fields?

Rhymes

A large and miscellaneous group of subjects, especially in children's folklore, is expressed in the form of folk rhymes. Many other forms of folklore also make use of the poetic device of rhyme; there are (as we have seen) rhymed proverbs and riddles as well as rhymed folk beliefs and rhymes in some games, customs, and folktales. Most of our present examples are children's play and game rhymes, simply because these have been the most collected in Utah. These tend to be short, simple, and apparently trivial, but if they are collected carefully and studied closely they may have considerable interest as folk poetry and for information on folk attitudes and psychology. Furthermore, a study of the minor variations in folk rhyme texts may help show us the patterns in which verbal lore varies as it passes in oral tradition.

The earliest folk rhymes a child learns may be the baby-bouncing and finger-play rhymes that adults use to amuse infants:

> *One, two, three*
> *The bumble bee.*
> *The rooster crowed*
> *And away he goes.*
> > *(Used by a grandmother when bouncing children*
> > *on her knee; collected Salt Lake City, 1969.)*

> *Knock at the door.*   *(tap the child's forehead)*
> *Peep in.*   *(lift eyelid)*
> *Lift up the latch.*   *(push up nose)*
> *Walk in.*   *(pop fingers in open mouth)*
> > *(Salt Lake City, 1967)*

As children grow older, they are taught nursery rhymes, and a few years later they may make up parodies of nursery rhymes to circulate among themselves:

> *Mary had a little lamb,*
> *You've heard it said before.*
> *Then she passed her plate again,*
> *And had a little more.*
> > *(Midvale, 1968)*

44

Many children's rhymes have overtones of ritual and magic about them, and may, indeed, be descendants of older magical chants. From Mammoth, Utah, comes this example collected in 1969 of a prophetic rhyme chanted by children when they saw a flock of pigeons:

One for sorrow,
Two for joy,
Three for a letter,
Four for a boy,
Five he comes,
Six he tarries,
Seven he courts,
Eight he marries.

The following example, even more ritualistic, is still very current as a means of limiting the membership in a group game:

```
Rhyme                              Amy Dixon
                                   Salt Lake City
                                   November 18, 1969


       Tick tock, the game is locked
       And nobody else can play;
       If they do, we'll take their shoe,
       And keep it for a week or two.

       (Before playing a game all of the kids gather
       around and hook arms, swing all their arms and chant
       this.)

                                   Susan Dixon
```

Photographed by Douglas Hill and William A. Wilson

Counting out with "one potato, two potato" rhyme

Counting-out rhymes, although they often sound mysterious, have no other apparent meaning than just a set of rhythmic syllables for choosing "it" for a game:

One re or-y,
Ickery Ann,
Phyllis-y follisy,
Nicholas John.
Queever quaver,
English neighbor,
Stinklum stunklum,
You be buck out.   *(Salt Lake City, 1969)*

45

Probably the most popular and common game rhymes of all are those used when jumping rope. Some of these rhymes tell a little story, and it is sometimes amazing how well they can sum up a typical childhood experience or point of view:

> *Johnny broke a bottle and blamed it on me,*
> *I told Mom, Mom told Pa,*
> *Johnny got a lickin', so ha, ha, ha.*
> *How many lickin's did Johnny get?*
> *(Jump and count until you miss.)*
> > *(Salt Lake City, 1968)*

> *Johnny and Sally up in a tree,*
> *K-I-S-S-I-N-G.*
> *First comes love, then comes marriage,*
> *Then comes Sally with a baby carriage.*
> > *(Salt Lake City, 1967)*

In other jump-rope rhymes the child jumping chants a rhyme in which he assumes a different personality or role. In some, as the following, he is expected to perform the actions mentioned as they occur in the rhyme, without missing a jump of the swinging rope:

> *I'm a little Dutch girl, dressed in blue,*
> *And these are the things I like to do:*
> *Bow to the captain, curtsy to the queen,*
> *And turn my back to the mean old king.*
> > *(Salt Lake City, 1967)*

In a modernized variant of this rhyme collected the same year, the little Dutch girl turns her back to "the washing machine."

Children sometimes put retorts, derision, and other aggressive commentaries into the form of rhymes. The following three examples from Utah are used to tease a redheaded person, make fun of a crybaby, and answer back someone who has called you an insulting name, respectively:

> *Gingerbread, redhead,*
> *Five cents a loaf*
> > *(Salt Lake City, 1967)*

> *Bawlbaby Tittymouse,*
> *Laid an egg in our house.*
> *Couldn't eat it,*
> *Had to keep it.*
> *Bawlbaby Tittymouse.*
> > *(Sandy, 1969)*

47

Jumping to jump rope rhymes   Photographed by Douglas Hill and William A. Wilson

```
Rhymed retort                           Steven Young
                                        Holladay
                                        July 27, 1967


       Twinkle, twinkle little star,
       What you say is what you are.


       (Two neighbor boys were playing.  Suddenly
    one jumped on his bike and headed for home chant-
    ing this as he went.  I didn't hear the name he
    was called, only the rhyme, and I recalled it
    when similar examples were given in class a day or
    so later.)


                                        Helen Ward
```

Some traditional rhymes are written rather than spoken, as in the following examples from a textbook flyleaf, autograph albums (two examples) and the coded rhyme from a mailing envelope:

If you steal this book, run for your life,
'Cause the owner carries a big jackknife.
> *(Salt Lake City, 1969)*

If this book should ever roam,
Box its ears and send it home.
> *(Sometimes used in textbooks as well as*
> *autograph albums. Salt Lake City, 1968)*

Can't think,
Too dumb,
Inspiration
Won't come.
No ink,
Bum pen.
Can't think.

> *Amen.*
> *(Midvale, 1968)*

PMPMDBS
BLEGMG
> *Meaning: Postman, postman, don't be slow,*
> *Be like Elvis, Go man go!*
> *(Salt Lake City, remembered from 1959)*

Folksay

Some rhymed epitaphs may be of folk origin. These may be collected by copying them down, photographing the tombstone, or making a rubbing with paper and dark crayon. The picture or rubbing is preferred if the stone has other interesting designs or inscriptions. Following are some tombstone verses from the Park City Cemetery:

Gone to a fairer land
Of pleasure and love
To join the bright band
Of angels above

Dearest John, he has left us
Left us, yes, forever more.
But we hope to meet our loved one,
On that bright and happy shore.

It came up on us by degrees
We saw its shadow, ere it kissed her.
The knowledge that our God has sent
His messenger for our sister.

Bright in Heaven's
Jeweled gown to shine
For ever more.

We have barely touched on a few subjects and forms of folk rhymes. To guide yourself to other examples of their use, these questions may be asked about your own experiences:

Do you know any parodies of nursery rhymes?

Do you know any rhymes referring to Utah, Mormonism, western life and scenery, or the like?

Are there any rhymed humorous, sentimental, or satiric epitaphs in local cemeteries?

Do people print commemorative rhymes in newspaper classified columns in your region?

What parody rhymes or poems do you know? How about parodies of hymns, scripture, poetry, or oratory?

Have you ever heard of rhymed recipes or other directions for making things?

Do you know any longer poems that circulate in oral tradition or as handwritten copies?

5

Folk Literature

Folk narratives, songs, and ballads are comparable in some ways to the short stories, history, poetry, and vocal music of formal culture. Instead of being written, published, recorded, or performed in concerts, they survive in oral tradition and in occasional accidental written versions, but they fill the same place in folk culture as their "higher" counterparts do at the "official" cultural level. *Legends* relate historical and pseudo-historical stories; *folktales* function as narratives of entertainment and moral instruction only, and *folksongs* embrace both lyrical expression and ballad narration. In a very real sense, then, these longer verbal forms of folklore may be thought of as a kind of literature of the folk. When we use such terms, however, we must remember that most of us are part of this folk and we possess some of this folk literature ourselves, whether in impressive forms like the Old World fairy tales and ballads, or in the less pretentious forms like jokes, anecdotes, game songs, or lullabies.

Legends

The term "legend" in a general sense refers to traditional historical narratives told as true, although in actual practice the tellers and listeners may not literally believe in them. Nevertheless, legends are usually linked to a specific actual locality,

Girls telling ghost stories   Photographed by Douglas Hill and William A. Wilson event, or person, and they are told as if a record of history, often in order to explain something, such as a place name, a geographic feature, or a bit of local history. Legends purporting to explain peculiar place names are a very common feature of American folklore, and they may circulate side-by-side with whimsical fictional explanations of the same names. In the following examples, the first is a legendary explanation for the place name "Hurricane," and the second is obviously a joke on the same name:

> *A group was travelling from Kanab to Cedar City, and they came to the fault, now called "Hurricane Fault." Indians were close behind, so they quickly lowered the buggies and the horses down on ropes. Two men went with the buggies and one remained behind on the cliff. A whirlwind struck the men in the buggies and they were whirled around and around, so they named the town nearby "Hurricane." The fault extends in a north-south direction near the town.*
> *(Salt Lake City, 1969)*

> *The place where Hurricane is now once was the Garden of Eden. Adam and Eve and their sons Seth, Cain, and Abel were travelling along. As they walked along Cain kept slowing down. Finally, one of them, I think it was Adam, turned around to see Cain straggling behind and yelled back to him, "Hurry Cain!"*
> *(Salt Lake City, 1968)*

Besides names for places in a state, the residents themselves may have nicknames with legendary explanations attached to them. Utahns are sometimes called "Carrot Eaters" or "Carrot Snappers," and carrots may be called "Utah (or Mormon) Bananas." Within the state, Sanpete County in particular is thought of as Carrot Eater country, a local saying maintaining that their biggest crops are "blonde babies and carrots." The blonde babies are the offspring of Scandinavians settled in that area, and some say the carrots are a favorite food of the Danes especially. Folk tradition can supply other answers: a Sanpete County child mistakes a banana for a carrot when visiting in Salt Lake, carrots are used to fatten pigs (hence "Carrot Eater" is an insult), and the story is told of a Sanpete man in a mine who kept eating the carrot used as a plumb bob when sinking and timbering a new shaft. It is not the place of folklore research necessarily to verify one or another of such explanations, but rather to collect all the variants and suggest what they convey about attitudes toward those to whom them are applied.

Folk legends are valuable particularly for the light they cast on the shadowy everyday concerns of the common people who are only statistics in most formal histories. It is not so much that these oral accounts may preserve fully factual data that is important, but that they present what seemed striking to the participants in events at the time in memorable form for their ancestors to inherit. Each age acquires a measure of folk history from the past, and from this — combined with present experience — it forges folk history for the future. This is not, of course, a conscious deliberate process, but a random and natural one in oral tradition. In Utah this has been an especially vital and ongoing matter, compared to other states. Utahns, still feeling a closeness to the scenes and personalities of their pioneer ancestors and encouraged by some of the tenets of the LDS church, display a lively interest in genealogy, family histories, pioneer artifacts, and documents of personal and regional history. Thus, the collector of local legends in Utah may easily find informants, young and old, with colorful stories like these to tell:

Local legend   *Kathy Kimball*
                                        (As learned from Belle Kimball)
                                        Salt Lake City
                                        November, 1967

A wagon train was coming through the Middle West on the way to the western territories. On the way a wagon broke down and the people had to discard almost everything. A flatiron was thrown out and the little girl of the family couldn't bear to have it left, and so she carried it all the way to Manti, Utah, from the Mississippi River. Everyone in Manti used the iron, borrowing it back and forth for many years. It was the only iron in the town for over ten years.

Arlene Pattison

An old man by the name of Luke Dewitt — one of the early settlers — he had some claims up above, up this gulch, and he'd walk up there and do his work on them and walk back down on the west side of the gulch. On this side was a ledge with a big quartz vein in it. And in the later years — along in the 1920's or something like that — he come down this gulch and this particular time he took that hillside and walked over that quartz ledge out there. And he happened to see where must've been somebody's hobnail; them old miners used them hobnailed boots. Someone had scratched the rock and made a streak of gold. He got a lease on it, and in just a little while he took out $8,000.00. It was just a little pocket.

Funny thing about that — they said the crew that was working just across the gulch, in the winter they'd walk over to eat their lunch in the sunlight, and set right on that ledge.

(Marysvale, 1969)

53

*My grandfather was the foreman, or anyway in charge, of the
stonework of the Temple, and my father who was about twenty-two
at the time was employed to cut stone. My father was assigned to
cut one of the lesser granite balls a-top the Temple today. This was
all done by chisel and hammer, hand hewn and polished so it took
time to do. My father became irked at the ball and gave the chisel
an extra hard jolt, and seemed to split the ball. But he was very re-
sourceful. He had just barely cracked it, and since it seemed quite
right structurally, he gave it to grandfather. It was put up on the
Temple, and it is still there today, but he always said that it would
be the first to fall and when it does he just hoped that no one would
be beneath it. (Salt Lake City, 1968)*

The subjects of local and historical legends need not extend back to the pioneers literally. The genealogical work that all Latter-day Saint families engage in
has produced a spate of anecdotes about strange coincidences, unexpected findings,
and humorous sidelines of research. For example, anecdotes about funny entries
on LDS Family Group Sheets either pass casually from researcher to researcher or
more formally in genealogical classes. Sample humorous entries are "I found my
grandmother crossing the plains in the library yesterday," and "Number seven child
died turning sumersaults and did not show up at the census." Such stories also pass
between workers at the Genealogical Society and the Church Welfare Office; a
welfare recipient is supposed to have written in, "How dare you say he is illiterate:
His father and I were married three months before he was born."

The legendary narratives we have seen thus far have been realistic and believ-
able, but a large group of folk legends deals with the supernatural. People tell of
haunts, omens, premonitions, witches, magic, monsters, and the like. Stories about
such subjects, which seem to be readily disproved by reason and ordinary experience, probe behind reason and into the unexplained wonders of the world and of
the human mind. The telling and further transmission of supernatural legends may
serve merely as entertainment, or may raise the questions "Can such things be?"
and "*How* can such things be explained?" The following story, for example, is a
typical Utah supernatural legend; it contains the familiar motif of the miraculous
or supernatural aid in a human task. (The informant's word for it was "imaginary.") It centers on the Mormon concern with genealogy, which can be a time-
consuming and frustrating task, but in which discoveries may be dramatic, unexpected, and seemingly supernatural. The setting and time of the story are wholly
modern:

54

*This one fellow had to go down to L.A. on business. He had
always been interested in genealogy, but too busy to do anything.*

> *After he'd finished his business, he had a free afternoon and decided to go to the Genealogical Research Library. Of course, everything being new he didn't know where to go or start. But as he walked into the library he saw an arrow — it wasn't painted or anything, it was imaginary — and he followed it down some stairs and down an aisle. It pointed at a book, and he picked up that book and found pertinent and necessary information that he needed in filling out his genealogy sheets. (Salt Lake City, 1967)*

One of the most distinctive and fascinating forms of folklore among Mormons is the body of supernatural legends concerning appearances of the Three Nephites. Three apostles of the Nephite people, according to the account in the *Book of Mormon*, were granted bodily life on earth by Christ until His Second Coming. Their mission is to save souls for the Lord, and they may appear, usually one at a time, to advise or assist Mormons in distress. Numerous accounts of supposed experiences with Nephites have circulated among Mormons in Utah and elsewhere for many years. Although some folklorists of the past have assumed that all Mormons believe such stories without question, and that the stories are declining in the modern age, folklorist William A. Wilson of Brigham Young University has shown by his recent field work that neither assumption is valid. (See his article "Mormon Legends of the Three Nephites Collected at Indiana University" in *Indiana Folklore*, II, 1969, 3–35.) In actuality, Wilson has shown, young people continue to tell the Nephite legends, but nowadays they are often told just to entertain.

Whether they are believed or not, whether from past history or the present, and whether told to increase faith, to question supposed supernatural happenings, or just to entertain, all legends of the Three Nephites still told in Utah ought to be collected. Even stories that obviously are adapted from other well-known legends or stories that only imply Nephite characteristics need to be studied in order to make it possible to judge clearly the influence and distribution of the Mormon subject matter in general Utah folklore. For example, the next story was collected from a Mormon girl, but the character in her story was non-Mormon. After relating the legend, the informant suggested that this might have been an instance of a Nephite intervention to help even a non-member of the Church, but she did not comment on the fairly unusual detail here of three helpers appearing at once. It should also be noted that although the story was collected in Utah, the setting is Arizona.

> *One night my girl friend was driving in the desert to Tucson, Arizona. She had forgotten to get gas and when she was on the highway she discovered that she did not have enough to reach Tucson.*

55

> *She was quite scared. She stopped her car and knelt beside it and prayed very hard to God that he would help her reach Tucson safely. She got back in the car and began to drive. About fifteen miles outside of Tucson she noticed a gas station. She was just running out of gas. She pulled in and had her tank filled. There were three young men at the station. When she arrived in Tucson she told her friends about the scare she had and how lucky she was to find that gas station open. They told her that she could not have possibly gotten gas there because that station had been closed for several years. She insisted that it was open that night. The following day she drove to the station with her friends. She was very surprised to find the station closed. It was a very old station and one could easily see that it had not been used in years. When they checked my friend's tank, however, they were all amazed to find that she had a full tank of gas. (Salt Lake City, 1966)*

Even a completely modern and urban setting may be the scene of a supernatural experience and provide the germ of a folk legend. This example, although incomplete as to the words or the purpose of the mysterious stranger, has the classic Nephite motifs of appearance, words of counsel, and sudden disappearance:

> *In Layton, in back of J. C. Penney's, there's only one entrance and one exit to the parking lot. As my daughter and her family pulled into the parking lot, a man came to the side of the car and took the baby by the hand. The man had long whiskers. He told my daughter some things concerning the baby. I couldn't tell you now what he said. I'd want it to be the truth, and I'm afraid I'd get the words wrong. So, I don't want to say. My daughter said, "One of the three Nephites!" Her husband said it almost at the same time, and the kids and all of them jumped out of the car and not one of them could see him. It seemed like he just disappeared. There was a river in the distance and there was no place he could have gone, but he was gone. (Salt Lake City, 1967)*

Urban legends tend to cluster around abandoned or run-down houses and cemeteries and their supposed haunts. Among adolescents such haunt stories are often told with a kind of semi-belief in order to frighten their friends and sometimes to initiate them into clubs and other groups. In Salt Lake City, where most of our collecting to date has been done, the best known haunt is Emo (or "Nemo") in the City Cemetery whose face, it is said, can be seen in the proper angle of moonlight. Other such scare stories worth collecting concern escaped maniacs, lost miners or prospectors, the ghosts of hoboes accidentally killed near railroad yards, and people crushed during tunnel, bridge, or building construction.

We have used the word "anecdote" in a general way without precisely defining it; what folklorists mean by the term is short, realistic, personal stories told as true. Among the most abundant anecdotes in American folklore, and plentiful in Utah, are those about local characters — lazy, stubborn, slovenly, crafty, or witty people — about whom little illustrative stories are told:

> *When the Uintah Basin first opened up there was only a few people out there and they usually had dances. There was this one old fiddler and he lived out on the range, and his wife passed away. So they advertised that there would be no dance that night. So, about dance time, here came the old fiddler. And they said, "Well, we postponed the dance because we figured that on account of your wife's death there wouldn't be any dance." And he said, "Well, I thought about it, and I thought about it, and I decided — Well, what's the difference, she was no blood relation of mine, so I might as well go and play the fiddle." (Salt Lake City, 1967)*

> *This guy came down to Eureka hunting a man to go to work on a mining project for him. A guy asked him what kind of man he wanted. He said, "I want a man big enough to run a windmus alone, dumb enough not to mind, and so damn ugly nobody will talk to him and stop him from working." Nobody was too eager to go to work for that kind of a man.*
>
> *(A "windmus" was an apparatus, usually cranked by two men, to lift ore buckets from the mine. Salt Lake City, 1969)*

> *There was to be an impressive tour given to some dignitaries from other lands. J. Golden Kimball was assigned to the tour as a guide. They first took a bus trip to the important historical sites in and around Salt Lake City. Brother Kimball would constantly remind the visitors how fast buildings were put up by the industrious Mormons. Every time he would say so, one of the dignitaries on the tour would say, "Oh, is that right? In our country we could do it in half that time." J. Golden Kimball began to get madder and madder as the dignitary persisted to offer such comments.*

> *The tour was to end by having the bus drive around Temple Square; then this dignitary asked, "What is that building there?" as he pointed toward the Temple. "Damned if I know," said J. Golden Kimball, "It wasn't there yesterday."*
>
> *(Salt Lake City, 1967)*

J. Golden Kimball

57

Questions for the collector of legends:

Can you collect any local explanations for place names? (No matter how inane they seem, do collect them, and get the variants too.)

Have you heard legends or anecdotes about notable or notorious Utahns like Brigham Young, J. Golden Kimball, Orrin Porter Rockwell, or Butch Cassidy?

Are there stories in your locality about Indians, hermits, madmen, prospectors, sheepherders, churchmen, political figures, or others?

Have you heard any accounts of appearances of the Three Nephites recently and orally?

Are there lost mines, dream mines, haunted houses, or other sites in your community about which legends are told?

Have you ever heard a story told as a means of verifying a superstitious belief in a cure, good or bad luck, an omen, or the like?

Do you know any legends related to geographical features or themes of the region — the Four Corners area, Grand Canyon and other national parks, mirages, thirst, exploration, or the like?

Can you collect *any* kinds of stories concerning fantastic animals, monsters, flying saucers, the Gadianton Robbers, ghost riders, the white steed of the prairie, healings, miracles, missionary experiences, or other remarkable or supernatural things?

Have you heard any stories of people whose spirits have left their bodies, visited the spirit world, and then returned, bringing with them valuable information about life "on the other side"?

Folktales

The distinction between legends and folktales is usually made on the basis of attitude: legends are regarded as historical, while folktales are obviously not true. But, as we have already seen, these criteria are not always workable. Some legendary narratives are believed by some people some of the time, but not all legends by all people all the time. Most anecdotal narratives are hardly meant to be taken seriously at all, yet they seem realistic and are clearly more like historical legends than fictional folktales. The situation with regard to folktales proper is similar; what a folklorist may recognize as a widespread fictional tale may be told in the manner of a local legend. The following example, for instance, is well known in Europe (it is even in the Grimm fairy tales), and yet it is adapted so well to the Utah setting (as it has been elsewhere in the United States) that it sounds exactly like a legend:

> *Down in Manti when the pioneers first went there and the temple was being built, they lived out in the rocks and sagebrush in their wagons and log cabins. One day one of the women found her little boy missing so she went looking for him.*
>
> *Pretty soon she heard his voice saying, "Some for you and some for me. Some for you and some for me."*
>
> *She walked around some rocks and there sat the child, feeding his sandwich to a rattlesnake. (Ferron, 1967)*

We seldom encounter the full-scale European folktales (erroneously called "fairy tales") in the United States except among immigrant families who have maintained some Old World customs or among settlers of British stock in fairly remote areas (such as the Ozark or Appalachian mountains where many long tales have been collected). At least for the immigrant stories, Utah would seem to be a likely collecting ground, but little has shown up so far. However, there are a few evident survivals of minor British folktale types to report. The *formula tale* — in this case a "round" — is known:

> *My two sisters are eight and nine years older than I. When I was a child I often asked them to tell me stories. Many times they would recite this one to me:*
>
> *"Twas a dark stormy night in December when into the bar staggered a stranger. The stranger's name was Alfonso. 'Alfonso, tell us a story!' Alfonso said, 'Twas a dark stormy night in December when into the bar staggered a stranger. . . .'"*
>
> *(Salt Lake City, 1969)*

Also, the following is one variety of a *pictorial folktale* popular in England and the United States to tell to children:

Pictorial folktale   *Michael Brugger*
Venice
November 12, 1966

> *This is called "The Mystery Pet." See if you can guess what kind of pet the old lady had.*
>
> *An old lady owned a big pond.*
>
> *There was a big island in the pond with grass on it.*

There were cattails at one end of the pond.

The old lady lived in a house with one window.

She shook her rugs out of the door.

There was a path that went from her house to the pond.

*Two Indians lived in tents and came up two
     paths each day for water.*

What was the old lady's pet?

*(A picture is drawn as the story is told, each detail being added as
shown above until the picture shown below is finished. The pet is
a big goose or other bird.)*

Geoffrey R. Brugger

    A distinctive American folktale type — though not without solid roots in European tradition — is the "tall" or "lying" tale, sometimes called the "windy." These are essentially jokes based on humorous exaggeration of real life situations. Since each *tall tale* tends to be based on one simple idea, they are sometimes reduced to one-line gags, such as these:

    *It was so hot around here in those days that we had to feed the
chickens ice cubes so they wouldn't lay hard boiled eggs.*
    *The Virgin River's so muddy that fish swim backwards to keep
the sand out of their eyes.*

60

> *Did you know that Brigham Young one time hired a man to drive a swarm of bees out here from the Middle West?*

The genuine flavor of oral tall tales is hard to render in print because so much depends upon the narrator's oral style and his deadpan expression; collectors must describe these features in detail. Try to imagine the following two stories as they were originally told by a southern Utah tour bus driver to his load of gullible tourists:

> *Going across this area you can see how dry it is, and you can see the many different colors that are in the hills. For this reason it is called "Prismatic Flat." Very little life exists on the Prismatic Flat, but you do occasionally see a few horses and a few cattle, but that's about all, and the cattle you see are real skinny and poor. As a matter of fact, some of these cattle are so skinny and poor that they can't even brand them, so they have to round them up and instead of branding them they get three of them and put carbon paper between them and stamp them with a rubber stamp.*
>
> *(Provo, 1968)*

> *Here on the Prismatic Flat it has been known to get so hot and dry that the jack rabbits have been known to kick the prospectors to death to get their canteens. In fact, the lizards on the highway take turns carrying one another piggy-back from white line to white line so they don't get their feet too hot. And even the trees out here, what few there are, call for dogs. (Provo, 1968)*

A characteristic device of the tall tale teller is to cast himself in the role of superman hero and narrate his big lies in the first person:

> *My parents was travelin' across the country to homestead and there was lots of Indians to look out for then, you know. Well, they made camp early 'cause my mom was pregnant with me then, and the mare she was ridin' was with foal. Well, during the night I was born and at that same time the mare give foal to a colt. Next thing we knew someone hollered, "Indians are comin'," so she jumped on the mare and I jumped on the colt and we outran the Indians! I was the youngest cowboy on earth. (Salt Lake City, 1967)*

Rendered as a third-person story, the tall tale sounds less plausible and therefore less interesting:

Tall tale

Kermit A. Peterson
Ferron
July 10, 1967
(He first heard it about 1955.)

61

> *There was this guy up camping at Ferron Reservoir. He was deer hunting. He had made his camp for the night and was laying there in his sleeping bag when he heard two voices:*
> *One said, "Should we eat him here or carry him home to the others?"*
> *And the other one answered, "Let's eat him here. He's too big to carry."*
> *The man looked up and saw two great big mosquitoes standing over him.*
>
> *Jane Warthen*

Since lengthy folk or "fairy" tales are rather rare, and tall tales are quite specialized, what does this leave for the average urban folklore buff to collect? The answer is *jokes*. Do jokes seem too common? That is all the more reason that they need to be written down and studied, for it is just the folklore that we are most used to and tend to take for granted that seldom gets recorded and analyzed. The fact that jokes *are* highly popular with people of all classes and all backgrounds suggests that they must have some vital functions to perform in modern life. A full discussion of the dynamics of joke-telling would take far more space than we have here, but let us glance at two Utah texts. The first joke is based on a typical parent-teacher-child encounter, and it ironically parodies the work of educational counselors and the tendency of over-anxious adults to seek complex answers to commonplace problems of growing up:

> *There was this little boy going to kindergarten, and it was one of those progressive type schools. He always drew everything in a black crayon, and the teacher was getting sort of worried about this because she felt that there was something wrong with a little boy who always drew everything with a black crayon. So she called in his parents and said, "I want you to look at these papers your son has been handing in. They're all just done in black crayon. I think you ought to take him to a psychiatrist and see what the trouble is."*
> *So the parents get an appointment with the psychiatrist and the little boy went and they were sitting there and the psychiatrist says to the little boy, "Son, now you've been turning in all these papers drawn in black crayon. Why do you do that?"*
> *And the little boy looked at him and said, " 'Cause it's the only one I got." (Salt Lake City, 1967)*

The second joke is surely of local origin. It demonstrates how in Mormonism (as well as in most other American religions) the practices of the faith can become the subject matter of traditional jokes. The threefold repetition, the economy of actions, the dialogue, and the climactic punchline are all typical of general American jokes, but the subject matter would not be fully understood without some familiarity with Mormonism. The informant here was a sixteen-year-old Mormon boy whose telling of the story seemed to reflect not his rejection of the Word of Wisdom requirements alluded to here, but his awareness of the difficulties of keeping them and the occasional pressures, even from fellow members, to break them:

> *Three Mormon elders were out on a camping trip, and on the third day they were all sitting around a campfire, and suddenly one of the men said, "Brothers, I must confess. Every night I've got to have a little nip." The others replied saying, "We know how it is." Then the second man said, "Since you confessed your weakness, I must. I've got to have a smoke every night." Then the other men replied again, "We know how it is." Then the third man spoke up and said, "Since you two confessed, I think it's my turn. Well, I gossip a lot, and I can't wait until General Conference."*
>
> *(Salt Lake City, 1968)*

Brief mention was made early in this *Guide* of Utah Indian folklore but only to explain why it is not covered. However, even though we must leave the native myths and legends for the linguistically-trained anthropologists to interpret, we should be on the lookout for legends and folktales about Indian-white relationships. This last example is a finely modulated social-protest story. It was collected by a white student from a Navajo co-worker on a job in Salt Lake City:

Folktale (Indian vs. white man)

Philip Lee Joe
Salt Lake City
November 20, 1966

> *An Indian and a white man were working on a big ranch and it was their day to play, and they were very hungry and sleepy. "I tell you what," says the Indian; "I saw a duck in a pond yesterday. Let's go kill him and eat him."*
>
> *"Okay," say the white, and they get their old guns and go after him.*
>
> *When they get to pond, Indian say, "Which will kill him?" "I will," says the white. "No, I will," says the Indian.*
>
> *"I tell you what," says the Indian, "we will both shoot him." So they do and they take him back to cook him and eat him.*
>
> *But he takes a long time to cook, and Indian says, "I tell you what. Let us go to sleep and the one who has the best dream will eat up the duck." "Okay," says the white, and they go to sleep.*

63

*But Indian sleeps with one eye open and he watches the white
and when he is asleep he goes and eats the duck all up. When they
wake up, the white says, "Okay, tell me your dream." "No," says
the Indian, you tell me yours first." "Okay," he say, "I dream that
I die and go to heaven and I met an old man and he told me to go in.
So I did and there was much food and I ate and ate, and I was
too full."*

*"That a good dream," say Indian, "and I have one like it. I
dream that I die and go to heaven too, but when I see old man he
say, 'Indian not allowed in heaven,' so I see you in there eating and
so I get hungry and come back and eat duck all up."*

Geoffrey R. Brugger

Ask these questions as you seek folktales in your collecting:

Do you know of any "Once upon a time" stories still passed on orally?

Are there immigrants in your community who tell "fairy tales" either in their native languages or in English?

Have you ever heard a tale or joke that had a rhyme or song as part of it? (Such stories are almost invariably European in origin.)

Can you collect tall tales about hunting, fishing, weather, animals, human exploits, machines, etc.?

Have you ever heard tall tales told to tourists to impress them with the wonders of Utah — perhaps on a guided tour or a chartered bus trip?

Do you know jokes about Utah, Mormonism, ethnic groups, well-known characters, current events, or the like?

Folksongs and Ballads

When most people think of folklore, songs come to mind first, but genuine oral traditional folksongs would seem to be the last things one might expect to collect in our contemporary mass-media dominated society. Americans associate folksongs with the long ago and far away — with minstrels and hillbillies, slaves and cowboys, nursemaids and grannies, and others of the past. Yet many songs still do circulate in oral tradition even with competition from records, radio, and television. Parodies of popular songs are one example; although usually short and silly, parodies are just as much a part of children's folklore as the songs of pioneer children. We quoted one folk parody of a well-known round in section one of this *Guide*, and here is another:

Row, row, row your boat
Gently 'neath the stream, [variant: "Underneath the stream"]

> *Ha, ha, fooled you,*
> *It's a submarine.* [*variant: "I'm a mermaid queen"*]
> > *(Salt Lake City, 1967)*

Oral parodies, it is true, have never been collected in large numbers as folk-songs, but there is no doubt that they could be. One reason for their neglect is that folklorists have inadvertently served as censors; they have hunted diligently only for the longer and more esoteric song types, ignoring the short and the common. But folk tradition contains many more parodies than the printed collections hint at, though parodies are usually quite well represented in folklore archives. Examples such as the following from the University of Utah archives indicate that earlier generations of children sang parodies of the popular songs of their own periods:

> *'Neath the crust of the old apple pie,*
> *There is something for you and for me,*
> *Though it may be a pin that the cook has dropped in,*
> *Or it may be a nice little fly;*
> *Or it may be an old rusty nail,*
> *Or the tip of the pussy-cat's tail,*
> *But what'ere it may be, it's for you and for me,*
> *'Neath the crust of the old apple pie.*
> > *(Mammoth, 1969)*

When people think of folksongs they have in mind something more dignified than parodies, and of course they are not wrong. American folk music includes many genuine treasures. Some types of songs, well known through recent professional singers and their recordings, are Anglo-American ballads and love songs, Negro spirituals, prisoners' work songs, and protest songs. Unfortunately for a current amateur collector in a state like Utah (and this is true of most states) few potential informants will be direct British immigrants, southern Negroes, prisoners, or members of a protesting mass movement. As a result, the songbag one fills is not likely to *seem* as worthwhile as one might have hoped or imagined. Not only region, but time works against us too; some twenty years ago Professor Lester A. Hubbard of the University of Utah scoured the state for folksongs and ballads and discovered a large and varied treasure of them, but where will we find today the counterparts of his then sixty- to ninety-year-old informants?

Instead of lamenting the loss of past traditions and giving up the folksong quest, we should become more aware of the singing of traditional music as it presently exists. The university students collecting in just the past few years in

Utah have proved that folksinging is still active here, and in some surprising ways.

Lullabies continue to be a popular form, and students have collected many examples for which published variants have not been found. Nonsense songs and other humorous types are known in some quantity, and children's game songs and teasing songs are very popular. Certain occupations — mining in particular — seem to have produced enough songs and singers in the past to penetrate even into the traditions of this age of highly mechanized mine work. One of the richest song traditions in the state centers on youth summer camps, whether religious, service organization, or just recreational camps. At camp, if not at home or in school, children learn songs orally from their leaders and their peers, and they sing them lustily around the campfires. They know rounds, endless songs, sentimental songs, songs celebrating nature and good fellowship, ethnic songs, songs for the dining hall, and satirical songs directed at each other's camp units (tents, cabins, patrols, etc.). Many texts and tunes have been collected, and more should be for an eventual full-scale study.

All folksongs have the obvious and important function of providing release and recreation through their aesthetic qualities. But songs may have other more positive social functions as well, such as unifying the rhythms of work groups, telling stories, pointing morals, inspiring religious faith, accompanying games, and the like. The following Utah song, from a student collection, with its brief contextual note has the special function of providing a lesson in local geography:

Mnemonic folksong

Student teacher
Salt Lake City
School year 1959–60

Utah Train

Beaver, Carbon, Davis, Morgan,
Dagget, Millard, and Duchesne,
Iron, Uinta, Rich, and Summit,
Garfield, Cash, Piute, and Kane.

Wasatch, Washington, and Weber,
San Pete, San Juan, Salt Lake, Wayne,
Juab, Box Elder, Grand, Tooele,
Sevier, Emery, Utah train.

(This is sung to the tune of "Ruben and Rachel." It was taught to me by a student teacher in a seventh grade social studies class as a way of remembering the names of the counties of Utah.)

Susan Weaver

66

Further texts of local folksongs, which are an important force in the building of the regional sub-culture, should be sought and collected. Although many of the songs of the Utah pioneers have been collected and published by earlier field workers, not much has been done more recently to determine whether the old songs are still transmitted orally or how they have varied between generations of singers. Utah songs and ballads such as "Echo Canyon," "Brigham, Brigham Young," "Blue Mountain," "St. George and the Drag-on," "Tittery-Irie-Aye," and "The Boys of Sanpete County" may be collected, as well as the localized parodies of more widespread songs ("Sweet Betsy from Pike," etc.) and recent compositions based on local events and scenes.

One of the common experiences of the amateur folksong collector is to stumble upon an interesting item (such as the one just quoted) when he least expects it. Seldom does a singer regard such a song as a "folksong"; it's merely a song so-and-so used to sing. The following verse was collected by a student from her mother, aged sixty-two, in Salt Lake City. Her mother's father had sung it to her as a child in New Jersey, and he had said he learned it when he was with the American army in the Philippines after the Spanish American War. It is still sung in the student's family; the stanza form and the tune suggest that it is based on a hymn:

> *There is a happy land,*
> *Far, far away.*
> *Where they have pork 'n' beans,*
> *Three times a day.*
>
> *Oh, how the boarders yell,*
> *When they hear that dinner bell,*
> *Oh, how the beans do smell,*
> *Far, far away.*

The distinction between folksongs and ballads is made on the basis of the texts' narrative contents: ballads tell stories, and folksongs express feelings, attitudes, or emotions. Since most songs of either kind at least *imply* some narrative, a further test is that the verses of ballads generally fit together in a set sequence, while folksongs tend to be more flexible and variable. However, as ballads pass on in oral tradition, the story line, as well as the words themselves, may become garbled. For collecting purposes, fine distinctions are unnecessary; the important thing is to record the material — both words and music, if possible. The following two folksongs (folklorists have not accepted variants of them as true ballads) clearly do tell stories, but they belong to a class of anti-feminist, anti-marriage

67

songs that scholars have regarded as lyrical rather than narrative. Both texts, it should be noted, frame the narrative content within stanzas of pure feeling:

Folksong   *Calvin C. Powell*
                                     Salt Lake City
                                 November 24, 1968

I Ain't Got No Use for the Women

I ain't got no use for the women,
A true one can never be found;
They'll use a man for his money,
When it's gone, they'll turn him down.

They're all alike at the bottom,
They're selfish and grasping for all;
They'll stick by a man when he's winnin',
And laugh in his face at his fall.

My pal was an honest cowpuncher,
Yes, honest and upright and true,
But he turned to a gun-shootin' gambler,
On account of a girl named Sue.

He fell in with evil companions,
The kind that are better off dead.
When a gambler insulted her picture,
He filled him full of lead.

All through that long night they trailed him,
Through sagebrush and thick chaparral,
And I couldn't help think of that woman,
As I saw him pitch and fall.

He raised his head up on his elbow,
The blood from his wounds flowed red,
He looked at his pals grouped around him,
He smiled and keeled over dead.

I ain't got no use for the women,
A true one can never be found;
They'll use a man for his money,
When it's gone, they'll turn him down.

(This was a song that was frequently sung by the students of North Summit High School of Coalville as they were transported from school to home on the bus. Calvin Powell, my father, age forty-six, learned and sang it in the years 1938 to 1940.)

Deborah Powell

68

Folksong

Calvin C. Powell
Salt Lake City
October 26, 1968

I Wish I was Single Again

I wish I was single again, again,
I wish I was single again.
For when I was single
My pockets would jingle,
I wish I was single again.

(All subsequent verses are constructed on the same pattern.)

I got me a wife, oh then, oh then . . .
She ruined my life,
And I wish I was single again.

My wife, she died, oh then, oh then . . .
I sat down and cried,
For I found myself single again.

I got me another, oh then, oh then . . .
T'was the Devil's grandmother,
And I wished I was single again.

She beat me, she banged me, oh then, oh then . . .
She swore that she'd hang me,
And I wish I was single again.

She got the rope, oh then, oh then . . .
My neck it did choke,
And I wish I was single again.

The limb did break, oh then, oh then . . .
My neck did escape,
And I found myself single again.

Young men take warning to this, to this,
Young men take warning to this.
Be satisfied with the first,
'Cause the second's much worse,
And you'll wish you were single again.

(This song was taught to my father by his mother when he was
a child at home on a farm in Upton.)

Deborah Powell

Folksongs on the same themes may be only superficially similar in attitude or phraseology, really constituting separate songs rather than variants of the same one. For instance, an informant may ask whether you know the song about wanting to be single again; if you answer affirmatively, thinking of texts like those just quoted, you may miss a new song such as the following one, which actually seems to be made up of fragments of two or three different songs:

When I was single, I lived at my ease,
Now I am married, a husband to please.
Two small children to entertain,
Oh how I wish I was single again.

One crying, "Mama, I want a piece of bread,"
One crying, "Mama, I want to go to bed."
Whip them, thrash them, send them to bed,
Listen while their father sings:

"I'm a comin' on a gray donkey,
Open the gates and let me come in.
What'll you give me? only a penny,
That is all I can afford."

Gypsy girls in paper dresses,
Gypsy boys in calico trousers,
If I had a bonnet, with red roses on it,
If I had a bonnet, I'd give it to you.

> *(Salt Lake City, 1969. The informant, age 58, learned it from her mother who had learned it from her father. Also she remembers her grandfather, who was from England, singing it to her when she was a small girl.)*

Folksongs of all kinds and in all conditions need to be collected. Do not wait to hear a better text from another singer, but write down everything that you hear. Here is a fragment of an interesting song commenting on a cowboy's life that one student was able to collect from an ex-cowboy, a co-worker in a local men's clothing store. (The last word in the third line is apparently a corruption of some other word, evidently a place name.)

Cowboy Song   *Dick Douglas*
                                                   Salt Lake City
                                                   February, 1970

One day I thought, I'd have some fun,
And see how punchin' cows was done,
So when around the Pary-gun,
I tackled a cattle king.
> *(four lines forgotten)*

They picked me up and carried me in,
And rolled me down with a rollin' pin,
And that's way they all begin,
"You're doing fine" says Brown.
"And then tomorrow if you don't die,
We'll give you another horse to try."
"Oh, won't you let me walk," says I,
"Yes, into town," says Brown.

I've traveled up and I've traveled down,
I've traveled this whole world around,
I've lived in cities, I've lived in towns,
But I got this to say:
Before you try it go kiss your wife,
Get a heavy insurance upon your life,
Then kill yourself with a butcher knife,
It's far the easier way.

(Mr. Douglas worked with the cattle drives in northwestern Utah
from 1917 to 1924. He states that there wasn't too much singing
of any kind, just when some "talent" arrived. Often times the cow-
boys would have great fun with a new hand, and this is what Dick
saw and also what this song deals with.)

John L. Powell

The songs regarded as the greatest prizes among American folklore collectors are those that descend from the British ballad tradition of centuries ago. Examples of most of these were published and discussed in the period from 1882 to 1898 by the Harvard ballad scholar Francis James Child in his book *The English and Scottish Popular Ballads*. Henceforth among scholars they have been known as the "Child ballads" and referred to by their numbers in Child's book. Never numerous in a collection, but always interesting, the Child ballads are often emphasized by being printed first in a published collection and by being analyzed more thoroughly by the collector than other folksongs. Hubbard, for example, in his Utah collection, has twenty-nine versions of nineteen different Child ballads at the beginning of his published collection of some 250 texts. The informant will not recognize his songs as Child ballads; it is unlikely he even knows the term, however rich his traditional stock of them may be. One student in 1970 sent back home to California for her mother's text of a song the student remembered her mother singing to her. Her mother, aged fifty-seven, had learned it from a family maid fifty years before in Salt Lake City. The maid was from Manti. Although the informant in this case had never before met anyone who knew the song or even who had heard of the song,

71

what she had in her memory was a text of Child ballad number 274, sometimes called "Our Goodman":

> *One night I came home late,*
> *One night, home late came I.*
> *And looking over the fence,*
> *Another man's horse I spy.*
> *"Whose horse is this," cried I,*
> *Whose ever can it be?"*
> *My wife she says it is a milk cow,*
> *That's what she says to me.*
> *Miles have I traveled,*
> *Scores or more,*
> *But a saddle on a milking cow,*
> *I never did see before.*

This version continues in the same pattern with these items: hat-flower pot-ribbons, boots-butter churn-spurs, shoes-chamber pot-laces, and man-baby-whiskers. For comparison, here is the opening of a Scottish version from a manuscript dated 1776:

> *Hame came our goodman, and hame came he,*
> *And then he saw a saddle-horse, where nae horse should be.*
> *"What's this now, goodwife? What's this I see?*
> *How came this horse here, without the leave o' me?"*

The sequence of items in this version is horse, boots, sword, wig, coat, and man.

The really classic British ballads are usually domestic or romantic tragedies, and rare though these are now in American tradition, one excellent text, previously unknown in this state, was collected in Utah, only weeks before these pages were written. Two students, Diane Peterson and Margaret King, made a tape recording on February 21, 1970, of the singing of Lucelle and Annamae Daly of Paragonah. Having sung several melancholy ballads, including one called "Silver Dagger," one woman remarked, "It puts me in mind of 'Two Brothers.' Now he [her father] used to sing that a lot too, and I learned it when I was very little. And let's do it for them . . . Now in this song, the first verse, there's a line that goes, 'Brother comb my sister's hair, as we go marching home,' which doesn't mean he's combing his sister's hair; it's a game they used to play. We never learned the game though." The song was then sung in unison to the melody indicated with guitar accompaniment:

The Two Brothers

Mon-day morn-ing go to school   Fri-day e'en come   home

"Broth-er comb my sis-ters hair as we go march-ing   home."

The Two Brothers

Monday morning go to school,
Friday e'en come home,
"Brother comb my sister's hair,
As we go marchin' home."

"Brother can't you play a game of ball,
Brother can't you catch a stone?"
"I am too young, I am too small,
Oh Willie leave me alone."

"You ask that I leave you alone,
I'll say that ne'er can be.
Oh I am the one who loved Suzanne,
And I will murder thee."

"What will you tell my mother dear
When she asks for her son John?"
"I left him in the country school,
A lesson for to learn."

"What will you tell my father dear,
When he asks for his son John?"
"I left him in the high wild wood,
A-learnin' his hounds to run."

Then he took out his little pen knife,
And it was keen and sharp,
With it he made a deadly wound,
That pierced him to the heart.

73

"Willie oh Willie go and dig my grave,
Dig it wide and deep.
Place the prayer book at my head,
And the hymnbook at my feet."

So he placed the prayer book at his head,
Hymnbook at his feet.
His bow and arrow by his side,
And now he's fast asleep.

Well might the singer be a little vague about the meaning of the line she commented on, for this text, though superior to many other American texts, somewhat disguises the story as it is told in the earlier Scottish versions from which it derives. Originally the motive for the fratricide seems to have been rivalry for a girl's love, possibly the sister's in an incestuous relationship. The first and third stanzas seem to retain traces of these details. Stylistic aspects of the older tradition include commonplace phrases ("little pen knife"), the heavy use of dialogue (in six out of eight verses), commands repeated in action (verses seven and eight), and the conventional roll call of relatives (verses four and five). The previously collected American texts which are closest to our Utah example were all collected in the Southern Appalachian Mountains in about 1916 to 1917, further testimony of the rarity of this particular survival.

What songs do you or your family know that you are not aware of having seen in print or heard on records, radio, or television?

Can you collect parodies of *any* songs?

Do old people of your acquaintance know some songs that younger people do not?

Are there local songs or ballads in your community that an outsider wouldn't know of? Are they related to history, occupations, or something else?

Do children sing teasing songs, game songs, parodies, or camp songs in your community?

Ask a child who has been to camp to list the titles of every song that he learned there from anyone at all.

6

Folklife

The concept of folklife is a European one which is only now gaining a following among students of American folklore. As the term suggests, folklife refers to the total traditional life patterns of a folk group — the customs, habits, rituals, beliefs, assumptions, arts, crafts, decorations, costumes, foods, and whatever else grows out of or is influenced by the group's traditions. In the past, American folklorists have studied some aspects of folklife, mostly folk beliefs, but they have failed to appreciate the importance of putting all elements into one composite picture of a traditional lifestyle. Following their own traditional practice of collecting *texts*, folklorists have slighted the social and cultural *contexts* in which folklore exists, and they have especially neglected the customary and material aspects of folk tradition. One irony of this is that whereas these neglected aspects of American folklore are highly visible and accessible, they are the least often studied and collected among the various types of folklore. In Utah, by way of example, hay derricks, rustic fences, and traditional granaries are prominent features of the rural agricultural landscape. Yet we have collected very little data about them, and we have less study of them than of Child ballads, which cannot be collected without a lot of luck, a lot of effort, or both. Within the short

A quilting bee   Photographed by **Douglas Hill and William A. Wilson** space and modest goals of this *Guide* we cannot hope to include a complete discussion of American, or even Utah, folklife; we can only describe the major areas in which material must be collected for the eventual studies. The ones we will survey are folk beliefs, customs, festivals, dances, and games, and the material folk traditions of architecture, handicraft, folk art, costume, and food.

Folk Beliefs

Folk beliefs, also called superstitions, include all those things that people believe, or act as if they believe, which cannot be rationally proved by logic or experiment and which are not part of the official teachings of an organized religion. In other words, folk beliefs — such as beliefs in divination, home cures, magic, luck, or witchcraft — step in where science and religion fail to provide positive results. Superstitious belief and practice are not limited to the naïve and foolish but rather have a strong grip on the otherwise reasonable senses of well-educated people. As one result, the "unlucky" number thirteen is often avoided in numbering floors and rooms in hotels, apartments, or office buildings. Many superstitious people felt a sense of justification when the flight of Apollo 13 in 1970 proved to be the most accident-prone space mission the United States had yet launched.

When collecting superstitions one should never refer to them by that name; no one ever thinks of himself as being superstitious. The first rule of interpreting superstitious behavior is not to trust the informant's self-justifications, though certainly these should be collected. A person may have any number of rationalizations for irrational behavior, but really only two basic reasons apply — it is traditional to do a certain thing, and one may feel more comfortable doing it. The essential reasons for studying superstitions at all are to observe how the mind works in response to day-to-day crises, and to see what kinds of traditional beliefs and practices are passed on in different variants.

The least useful kind of folk belief collecting is that which simply paraphrases an idea such as "A black cat crossing your path is bad luck" and names the source. What we want to know is how such an item comes up in daily life, what behavior (if any) follows from it, if it is believed, if it is passed on, if it is known in variants, and the like. Here is the same basic item of demi-belief as two different students collected it; both describe the context well, but the second also includes both her own and her informant's responses to the item:

78

Last Christmas I was going to send my aunt and uncle a set of steak knives and my mother said she wondered if my aunt would

send me a penny in return, "or maybe that doesn't work with rela-
tives." I didn't know what she was talking about, so she explained,
It's bad luck to give knives as gifts because they cut friendships.
So usually the recipient will give the donor a penny so they're pur-
chasing it instead of being given it. That keeps the friendship from
being severed, supposedly." But she didn't send the penny to me,
though she told me later that she knew about the superstition.

(Salt Lake City, 1968)

Doctor ———— is an obstetrician-gynecologist in Salt Lake
City. When we were at her home last April she gave my mother a
disposable scalpel which she said was excellent for picking seams
when sewing. But she refused to give it to Mother unless Mother
gave her a penny in return. She said that when a person gives a
friend a sharp-edged gift, a penny must be given in return or the
friendship will be cut. She had lost two or three very good friends
because she hadn't followed this rule. I was surprised to find some-
one this well educated who apparently believed such a thing.

(Salt Lake City, 1969)

As a general rule, superstitions cling the hardest to the riskiest or least predict-
able human problems or activities, and they often contain within themselves their
supposed explanations. Gambling, for instance, is risky and impossible to predict,
at least without cheating. Thus, gamblers are notoriously superstitious, whether
as a matter of literal belief or just traditional practice. An example:

It is good luck when playing the slot machines to leave a few
nickels, dimes, or whatever the specific machine pays off, in the
pay-off tray. Apparently the money in the machine is attracted to
the money in the tray. I don't really believe this, though I always
do it when playing a slot machine. (Salt Lake City, 1967)

Most other endeavors involving risk will attract some superstitions. This is
true whether the activity involves actual physical danger (military combat, race car
driving, rodeo riding, steeplejack work, etc.) or potential loss of freedom, money
or property (business, farming, crime, etc.). The dangers need not be very intense
for superstitions to develop. Bridge players, for example, are often fairly intense
about their lucky practices:

I always try to put my table at an angle, kitty-corner to the bath-
tub, when I play bridge because the good hands always go with the
bathtub. That way neither side gets all the good hands.

(Salt Lake City, 1967)

79

*Last December four of us were playing bridge and the first
time a 2, 3, and 4 came out on an ace, one guy muttered "Wish
Trick." Since I considered anything worth a try, every time a wish
trick came out I wished I would get engaged. That same night at
11:00 Bob gave me a diamond. (Salt Lake City, 1968)*

The folklore of wishing could be a study in itself — the occasions when wishes
are made, which ones may come true, rituals to guarantee a wish, rhymes that
go with wishing, and the like. One student collector described the "wish chip"
which is a potato chip which is folded completely over. It must be eaten whole
while the wish is made. Others described wishing on the odd-shaped kernels in
nuts, seeds in fruit, unusual sights, and upon finding certain things. Sometimes
wishing is an alternative to bad luck when a certain thing occurs, as in this interesting example:

*I was having lunch with a friend when she noticed me turn the
clasp of a necklace which had worked its way around to the front so
that it was again at the back of my neck. She said, "You know, you
should never do that. It will give you bad luck." She explained that
you must wait until the clasp is touching whatever is hanging on the
front of the necklace (locket, etc.), make a wish and then move
the clasp to the back of the neck. The wish is supposed to come true.*
(Salt Lake City, 1969)

```
Superstition                            Frank Nolan
                                        Logan
                                        November 15, 1968


     If you drop a knife, step on the handle with the
left foot or you will burn yourself when you are cook-
ing, or you may cut yourself.

     (He told me this was actually practiced in the
kitchen where he worked.)

                                        Jacqueline Nason
```

The pattern in superstitious behavior seen in the above examples is the sequence of (1) omen, (2) undesirable result, (3) counteraction to avoid the result.

With many items of superstitious practice, however, there seems to be no apparent explanation at all. It is simply something one does, has always done, and passes on to the next generation.

Superstition   Juanita Morris
                                     Salt Lake City
                                     October 22, 1968

    Whenever my grandfather had been working all day
in the field and was really tired--when he'd come
home at night, he'd stick one shoe inside the other
and put it under his bed. And that made it so he
wouldn't toss and turn at night and he'd sleep well.
I have three aunts that still swear by this.

                                     Linda Davidson

Instead of merely collecting assorted superstitions from daily life in scattered examples, one might concentrate on all the available superstitions concerning one subject. This practice is more useful for study purposes. Some areas of life that are likely ones for collecting in Utah include weather prediction, hunting and fishing, planting and harvesting, animal husbandry, travel, and certain occupations such as mining, construction work, and manufacturing. Another approach is to concentrate on the practices associated with the cycle of life — birth, death, baptism, courtship, marriage, and so forth. With a collecting project of this kind one should not limit himself to taking down what informants admit to believing in, or he will collect very little. The complete collection should contain all of the items of folk belief that are known — whether believed and practiced or not — plus observations of unconsciously superstitious behavior, such as knocking on wood, crossing the fingers, doing things in a certain order, and the like. Another important technique is to return to informants several times to ask them whether they know the

81

beliefs similar to theirs collected from others. Later, one might draw up a questionnaire to assure that every informant from the folk group is asked to comment on the same examples; this questionnaire then may be revised to allow for later data.

The folklorist studying superstitions should collect all variants, however minor, of each kind of item that interests him. The larger his basic assemblage of data is, the more he should eventually be able to say about his subject. Let us examine one area of Utah folk belief with these principles in mind, that of traditional home cures, especially those for removing warts.

Although several hundred cards containing folk remedies are already on file in the University of Utah Folklore Archives, doubtless the collection is far from complete. Home remedies extend back in time to the pioneer period, and a great number, judging from the massive collections made in other states, are still practiced. The items collected by students in Utah thus far have been sorted according to the ailments, and some fifty different ones are represented, ranging from bee stings and nosebleeds to cancer and pneumonia. As one might expect, the diseases and ailments least effectively treated by medical science are those most commonly associated with folk remedies; there also seems to be a correlation between the ailments common to old age and the use of folk cures. In alphabetical order, the specific conditions most often mentioned in this particular collection are arthritis, colds, coughs, earaches, hangovers, hiccups, rheumatism, sore throats, and warts.

From 1966 through 1969 some forty instances of folk remedies for removing warts were turned in, and there are virtually no exact duplications, which suggests that the collection is still incomplete. Warts, it might be pointed out, seem to come and go in a mysterious manner, so they are prime subject matter for superstitions. The traditional prescriptions for wart removal seldom specify any definite period of time before the wart disappears, so it is easy to conclude that whatever one has done to remove a wart may eventually work. Skimming through the various Utah wart cures, we find them ranging from outright magic to plausible procedures. (The place of collecting for each item may be assumed to be Salt Lake City, unless otherwise stated.)

Warts are often alleged to be caused by handling frogs, and one countermeasure is to touch a toad to remove them (1967). Another idea is to kill a frog and bury it under a full moon (1967). Several folk ideas are more like homemade surgery than magic: one should stick a needle in the wart nightly for a month, cut cross-shaped slashes in it with a razor blade, or touch it with a hot match end (all 1967).

82   The majority of folk ideas for wart removal involve rubbing something on the

warts: castor oil (1967), olive oil (1969), dandelion or milkweed sap (1967), soda and vinegar (1968) or saliva. When saliva is used, it is supposed to be applied by licking a finger and wetting the wart just before eating (1969) or upon first waking up in the morning (1967). Often the rubbing is followed by burning the item that was applied to the wart, whether a bean (1967, 1969), black-eyed peas (1967), or a potato (1967, 1968, 1969). Sometimes the ritual is fairly complex: one rubs the bean on the wart, spits on the bean, closes his eyes, and throws the bean over his left shoulder (1967).

Dishrags and potatoes are most often reported as things to rub on warts to remove them, and both of these items tend to be surrounded with other magical charms to make them work properly. Generally the dishrag must be stolen, rubbed, then buried secretly; when the rag rots, the wart dries up. The dishrag must be old and dirty, maybe even rubbed first in bacon grease (1969), or a piece of bacon may be substituted (1967). The rag may have to be buried by the light or dark of the moon (both 1967), or it may be hidden instead of buried (1967). Some say that if the rag is found (1969) or if someone sees you bury it (1968) the magic will not work.

The potato rituals are similar to the dishrag ones. Usually an old or even a rotten potato must be used. It is touched to or rubbed on the wart, and then buried or thrown away or given to one's mother (Richfield, 1967) to be thrown away. The potato may have to be spit upon before rubbing (1968) or first cut in two equal halves (1969). In one report only the peel of a potato is used (Tooele, 1968). Two informants quoted a verbal formula to say while disposing of the potato: "I commit you to the earth" (1966), or "Moon, moon, please take my warts away" (1969).

Pure ritual magic without any possible curative juices from rags or potatoes or other items are also found. One student's grandmother "counted" his warts away by rubbing each one and chanting some words (not understood) over them (Tooele, 1968). Another informant used a carrot to rub with, but the magic was effected by cutting a piece from the end of the carrot each time it was used; as the carrot disappeared, so did the warts (1968).

A hair from one's own head may be tied on a wart to make it go away (1967). More commonly used in "tying" cures is string, either just knotted once per wart (1968) or knotted, dampened, and buried to rot away, taking the warts with it (1967).

Finally, one may urinate in the middle of a road to remove his warts (1969), rub a new penny on the warts (1969), or sell them. If one wants to preserve the buyer from actually getting the warts, he should throw the money that is received away, and whoever finds it then gets the warts instead (Farmington, 1967).

Taken separately, none of these wart cures says much about folk psychology or traditional belief. But viewing the larger group we can readily see some of the themes of symbolism, ritual, and magic that run through them. Warts are symbolically represented by warty animals, knots, and root vegetables. They are ritually touched, rubbed, tapped, wet, cut, pricked, burned, or counted, and verbal charms or moonlight may assist in their removal. Like influences like, so that a rotting string or rag and a gradually cut up carrot causes the wart similarly to vanish. Warts are transferred by selling and through contact with other persons or substances. They may have some connection to other parts or products of the body — hair, saliva, or urine. Secrecy, theft, and stealth may be employed in their removal. The total picture — at least as we can see it now — shows that warts, though harmless and relatively inoffensive bodily growths, are still associated with fear, mystery, and magic in the minds of many people. It is likely that as more instances are added to our collection the picture will become clearer.

As can be judged, even from our short treatment, the field of folk belief is immense, and we can only suggest a few more questions to use in field collecting.

What does it mean if you sneeze, if your nose itches, if silverware or a dishcloth is dropped, or if a bird flies into the house or against a window?

What are some good general home remedies and tonics?

When can you wish and have it come true?

What foods are made at certain times, or eaten at certain times, by certain people or with special precautions?

What does it signify if a person puts a hat on a bed or gets some clothing on inside out or backwards?

What do you do if your car passes a cemetery or crosses railroad tracks or goes through a tunnel?

What folk beliefs or practices are associated with birth, death, or marriage?

What *predicts* rain or snow, and what *causes* rain or snow?

When do you plant, slaughter, harvest, preserve, etc. on a farm or ranch?

What must one *avoid* doing or saying in certain circumstances?

What beliefs and practices separate the boys from the girls?

Can you report on the carrying of amulets and other lucky charms or the use of doodle bugs, water-witching wands, and other magical items from your region?

Customs

Customs are traditional habits, actions, practices, and rituals, which are performed mainly because they *are* traditional. People expect certain customary behavior, and they rely on it to take place in specific situations. There are no rules attached to customs; nonetheless, they are often practiced with all the care and seriousness of obeying civil or moral laws. Customs may vary a great deal from region to region or family to family, or they may be fairly regular concerning a particular subject throughout a whole culture. The only scientific way to study customs is to begin with the assumption that they are all arbitrary and conventional. One's own customs are not "right" and others' are not "wrong." They are simply different. The extent to which customs correspond between areas of tradition may only be determined from careful collecting and comparative study. Here, for example, is an account of who customarily pays for what in a formal wedding, as compiled by a Utah student in 1969. How well does it describe the practices you know, and what variations are you aware of?

Father of the bride:	*Renting the church*
	Church music
	Minister's fee
	Wedding reception
	Flowers
	Bride's dress
	Invitations and announcements
Groom's family:	*Rehearsal dinner for wedding party*
Groom:	*Engagement and wedding rings*
	Honeymoon
Bride:	*Groom's ring*
	Bridesmaids' gifts
Bridesmaids:	*Their own dresses*
Ushers:	*Their own tuxedos*

The basic American wedding customs are well known: there is traditional clothing, music, seating of guests, opening and displaying of gifts, prank playing, kissing of the bride, tossing of the bouquet, throwing of rice, and so forth. But within groups who are influenced by special regional or ethnic traditions, there may be a good deal of variation on these practices, as well as some wholly different ones.

One Austrian custom, for example, is still practiced in Utah, and there are several other European immigrant groups here that have similar customs.

```
Custom                                    Pete Blansky
                                          Helper
                                          Fall, 1969

    At the wedding party all male relatives and
bachelors get to dance with the bride, for a price.
They have to pin at least a dollar bill on the bride's
dress.  The object is to get all the bachelors out to
participate.  This is supposed to be a custom of the
Austrians in this area.

                                          Kathleen Giacoletto
```

Many customs are associated with other personal celebrations (birthdays, graduations, anniversaries, promotions, etc.) or crises (childbirth, illness, accident, death, etc.). Often the customs for special occasions are linked to folk belief, as when the customary blowing out of birthday cake candles is associated with good luck or wishing, or the stopping of clocks when someone dies is associated with avoiding offense to the spirit of the dead. Even when there is no conscious sense of superstition involved, as when a bride neatly and economically avoids breaking ribbons on her presents, there may be a folk belief underlying the action (broken ribbons mean bad luck, or babies, or fights with her husband). Thus, customs and superstitions — actions and beliefs — are often collected as one item.

Customs may be adapted to fit in with other aspects of a subculture. In Utah, for example, the customary giving out of cigars to announce the birth of a child is sometimes substituted among Mormons by giving candy or bubble-gum cigars. The customary term "coffee break" remains in use locally, even if the participants drink hot chocolate or milk. Some customs are stereotyped in rigid commercial form, such as when customary American hospitality toward newcomers is taken over by "Welcome Wagon" and Christmas trees are manufactured of plastic or metal. On the other hand, new customs develop to go with new activities; thus, we have traditional family patterns for television viewing, naming practices for spacecraft, and whole new lifestyles among revolutionary groups.

To the participants themselves, customs never seem to be "special" or even deliberate. "That's just the way you do it!" people will insist. A Salt Lake student described the birthday party customs associated with the cake and candles this way:

> *The birthday cake is decorated with small candles, each year represented by one candle. After a person begins getting older he usually doesn't put the total number of candles on his cake, either because he doesn't want to admit his age, or because there simply isn't enough room. In that case, two or three candles are used. The cake is presented with candles lighted, and the person whose birthday it is makes a wish and blows the candles out. If the candles are blown out in one breath, the wish comes true.*

But other students in the class added different details and raised questions from their own experiences. What about the number of tries it takes to blow out the candles? Who cuts and serves the cake? Are there any extra candles on the cake? Is there a silence taboo until the birthday person has eaten his first piece of cake? Questions of this kind covering the entire pattern of birthday celebration are posed by the questionnaire at the end of this *Guide*; you are invited to fill it out and send it in to the Utah Heritage Foundation. By this means we may survey the customary practices associated with one special event over the entire state. Similar questionnaires might be created to study such customs as those associated with the loss of baby teeth, graduation, dating and engagement, showers for brides and mothers-to-be, and the like.

Personal and family customs have very seldom been collected because the general reaction of informants, and even collectors, has been "Is *that* folklore too?" Indeed it may be. Consider the question of tipping waitresses, for one example. How much does one leave behind? The etiquette books differ on the answer, and their recommendations change with the times. Individuals follow different lines of reasoning, some even deciding to leave no tips at all. Where does the folklore come in? Wherever there is some traditional idea or practice and some variation. What percentage of the total bill should the tip be? Where on the table is the tip to be left? What is said to the waitress? What do different denominations of cash signify? In Salt Lake City an informant said that leaving a dollar and a penny as a tip means good service; hopefully, the waitress for an expensive dinner will know this.

87

Some customs may be completely personal, or limited to a single family. Without more collecting, it is impossible to tell if this is the case or not with an item like the following, where again there seems to be underlying superstition involved as well:

```
Custom                                    Margery Faulkner
                                          Ogden
                                          November 7, 1969

    Whenever we leave the house for a trip or a
vacation, we have to get the house "in dying order."
This includes cleaning the oven, but we are usually
neither ambitious nor superstitious enough to
actually clean it.  We do always see that the house
is straightened, beds made, bathrooms clean, dishes
done.  My mother said her mother would never leave
the house for any reason until it was "in dying
order," but the custom only applies to vacation
trips in my mother's case.

                                          Marianne Faulkner
```

Other customs are widely known and standardized; traditional hand gestures are an example. Nearly every American, from school age on up, probably knows what is meant by crossing the fingers, pointing a thumb down with the fingers closed, holding the nose, thumbing the nose, or pretending to slash the throat with one finger. New uses of traditional gestures have quickly become current, such as the V-sign changing from "victory" to "peace" in the past few years. Other gestures are used as part of group work, such as railroading, aligning fences, or officiating sports events. Among returned LDS missionaries in Utah some interesting collections have been made of gestures learned in the foreign mission fields. Gestures used for ritual identification in closed groups may also be studied.

Calendar customs are those associated with holidays, and again there is a national norm and a good deal of regional variation. One good project is to compile a "folk calendar" for a particular group, giving the complete list of all holidays of the year that are celebrated and the customs that are practiced during them, particularly those that are local, ethnic, or unusual. Here one must distinguish the commercial and school sponsored customs (like Valentine's Day card exchanges) from those that are folk and traditional (like April Fool's or Halloween pranks). Following is one example of a family Christmas custom from Utah:

> *This tradition started in my home when the children no longer believed in Santa Claus and it has carried through our family for years. On Christmas Eve, after dinner, we would put all the presents in several piles, according to whom they were for. We placed them upside down, so that no one could see who they were from. Then each of us would be allowed to pick one present to open, but only one. The rest went under the tree for in the morning. One person at a time would open his present. (Salt Lake City, 1969)*

There are many questions that can be asked about individual customs, but the following may serve as a beginning:

What customs are associated with special events such as birthdays, engagements, weddings, births, graduations, or funerals?

How do you distribute gifts at birthdays or Christmas?

Do your family or your friends observe any special holiday customs?

What do you do on April Fool's Day, Valentine's Day, Halloween, May Day, Memorial Day, etc.?

Are there customs in your family or community handed down from pioneer times?

Do you know customs associated with giving or receiving gifts, lending tools, playing games, or taking examinations?

How do you choose sides for starting different games?

Have you ever taken part in a shivaree?

What customary practices are involved in hunting, fishing, skiing, or other sports and recreations?

What specific practices distinguish a Mormon wedding from others performed in Utah?

Festivals and Dances

Under this heading we can only raise a few questions and offer some generalizations based on research in other regions, for the collecting of descriptions of festivals and folk dances in Utah has not ever really begun yet. But there is such a strong history of unified group effort in settling this state, and there are so many general traditions of socializing and working together, that there seems little doubt that the group participation traditions of folk festivals and dances must have been

89

rich in Utah and in some instances at least may still be collectable or even observable here. These two terms refer to whole communities or other large folk groups working together, playing together, or celebrating together in traditional ways.

Perhaps the basis of many American festivals was the pioneer work group — a special gathering of friends and neighbors to pitch in and help finish some important big job. The task may have been some necessary stage of settlement, such as clearing land, house raising, painting, branding, or harvesting. Or the job may have been a domestic one like quilting, husking corn, or preserving food. Other special gatherings of folk were for activities like rabbit drives, auctions, spelling bees, or elections. As such occasions became periodic affairs, they developed a protocol to establish who called the group together and how, what work was done, what hours were worked, who fed the workers, how they relaxed and rested, and so forth. Pranks and contests became an integral part of the activities, as when men on harvest crews played tricks on each other or a man finding a red ear during a corn husking could kiss the girls. Gradually the first necessary work groups developed into more recreational festive occasions. The threshing gang may have turned their gathering into a local harvest celebration; the quilting bee became a church social event; the rabbit drive was more important as a time to hold a big dance than a time to eradicate pests. It has been suggested that the term "hoe-down" for a lively dance derived from the chance to put down the hoe and have a ball.

When such traditional diversions become highly organized and officially sponsored, they cease to have much, if any, connection with folklore. Such would seem to be true of today's county fairs, rodeos, and Arbor Day celebrations, to list only three examples. But in small communities genuine folk festivals still linger on, connected perhaps to some special local crop or occupation or ethnic settlement.

Certain recreational activities would appear to be likely ones about which folk practices still remain. Hunting, fishing, river running, and mountain climbing, for example, all involve a degree of group effort and cooperation. Are there special traditional elements connected to these? How is the game divided for a hunting party? Who sits where in the boat or gets the best location for the hunt? What is the protocol for camp tasks? Are new members of the group hazed or initiated? Is there any ceremony for opening summer cottage areas in the spring and closing them in the fall? In Utah, family reunions are at least partly folk festivals. The times and places they occur, the speechmaking, foods, entertainment, and other elements all eventually take on a stereotyped pattern year after year. Another gathering to study is the missionary farewell party.

90

Folk dances were often an important part of festive occasions or were perhaps in themselves the main occasion. In either case, this is a convenient place to call attention to the need for collecting them.

One old-time dance form that still survives in some children's groups was the *play party*. This was a group dance, often with a dramatic element, done to the tune of unison singing by the whole group. "Skip to My Lou," "Weevily Wheat," and "Let's All Go Down to Rouser's" were three early American favorites. The explanation is sometimes given that play parties were invented because preachers forbade fiddle playing at dances, but it would appear that both "playing" and dancing were popular in the same communities, along with instrumental music itself. More likely, play parties were developed for those times when no instrumentalists happened to be available for a dance.

Only a few play parties have been collected so far in Utah. One that exists in two variants is now known only as the children's game "Roger is Dead" or "Old Humpty is Dead"; it begins:

> *Old Humpty is Dead and gone to his grave,*
> *Gone to his grave, gone to his grave.*
> *Old Humpty is dead and gone to his grave,*
> *He, Hi, Ho, Hum.*

All the players join hands in a circle and either all together act out the remaining verses of the song or watch two players act them out in the center of the circle. In the song, Old Humpty has an apple tree planted on his grave, the apples ripen and fall down, and an old woman comes by picking them up, whereupon Humpty whacks her or kicks her away.

Another charming text of a play party song was collected by a student from her eighty-five-year-old grandmother in Salt Lake City. The informant's mother, who was brought to the city from Denmark when she was eleven years old, was an orphan. She was raised by a well-to-do Mormon family and lived for one period in Brigham Young's household. When and where she learned this typical Anglo-American play party game is unknown, but it has now passed down through three more generations:

> *Wally, wally, wallflower,*
> *Growing up so high,*
> *We are all young ladies,*
> *And we are sure to die.*

91

All except Miss ———— [name of one player]
She's the fairest flower.
She can't hop, she can't skip,
She can't turn the candlestick.

Fie, fie, fie for shame,
Turn your back and tell his name.
———— [boy's name] is a nice young man
He came to the door with his hat in his hand.

He asked if Miss ———— was in,
She's neither in, she's neither out,
She's up in the parlor walking about.

Down she came all dressed in silk,
A rose on her bosom as white as milk.
She walked to the door and bade him come in.
Tomorrer, tomorrer, the wedding will begin.

Tomorrer, tomorrer, the wedding will begin.
Go wash her in milk,
And dress her in silk,
And write her name down in gold pen and ink.

One 1967 summer school student at the University of Utah, Lois Lunt Metz, of Oakland, California, has written down from her memory the dance steps and tunes of popular dances she knew around Nephi in the 1920s. Here is her account of an unusual item from 1921:

> *When I was in my teens, I used to chord on the piano for an old-time fiddler in Nephi, Utah. He just fiddled along on the violin and yelled out the chords I should play: "Key of C," "Key of G," and so on, and I would play the chords that fit the melody. This is one tune that I have written down from memory.*
>
> *This tune was memorable because the fiddler would play until he reached the place in the music where the words, "Fire! Fire! Fire! Fire!" are; then he would stand up, hold his fiddle and bow up in the air, and yell out the four words. When he would do this, you can well imagine the pandemonium in the dance hall until the people came to recognize the tune. Then it caused a big laugh. He would go on playing, and the people would go on dancing. The music went like this:*

92

Fire! Fire! Fire!

(yell) Fire! Fire! Fire! Fire!

(yell) Fire! Fire! Fire! Fire!

We need to collect a great deal more information about Utah folk festivals and dances, and we may begin with projects like these:

Describe any work group traditions or local celebrations that you know of. Try to write a historical sketch of each one. (Can anyone describe a prison work group and its products for you?)

Quilting is still common in Utah, but to what extent have quilt patterns, names, or work methods been handed down traditionally from generation to generation?

Are roundups, brandings, or other cattle jobs done by ranchers' work groups in your area?

Can old people describe play parties and old-time dances, and do young people still do them in your area?

Do you know of any immigrant or Indian festivals or dances?

What folk elements are there in the Utah celebration of Pioneer Day and centennials?

Games

Folk games are mostly children's own unselfconscious traditional recreations, those that are not learned from teachers or playground directors or played with commercial equipment according to printed rules. A few recreations that qualify as folk are also passed from adults to children or make use of some manufactured items. Among strictly adult groups folk games are uncommon, although the traditional sport of hazing newcomers is practiced in some occupations.

The collection and study of folk games casts light not only on the variations of texts and actions that have passed from generation to generation traditionally, but also on the maturity development of growing children. Through their natural play children are partly educating themselves for roles in adult life where similar tasks and rewards will be encountered. The structures, symbols, and stresses of their games constitute a model of some adult challenges. The value of games and role playing in formal learning situations, in fact, has recently begun to be appreciated by educators themselves. Such generalizations as these apply readily to such games as "Mother May I," "Stone School," or "Cops and Robbers," but they are equally valid, if less obvious, in most other games as well.

A simple but familiar form of folk recreation is the *pastime*, distinguished from true games by the lack of winning or losing. Making string figures ("Cat's Cradle"), bouncing balls, juggling, and blowing bubbles are all pastimes. Another frequently collected in Utah is making toys or dolls from a folded handkerchief; this is often done to keep small children quiet during church services. (A related folk art is the "quiet book" mothers sew for their children.) A simple pastime puzzle can become a game if two or more players compete in solving it.

Children's games involve physical action, manipulation of objects, and mental activity, often all three in a single game. In the game "Lemonade" (or "Dumbies' Trade"), for example, two teams are chosen and they line up facing each other. They exchange a dialogue like this:

1st: "Here comes a jolly butcher boy looking for a trade."

2nd: "What is your trade?"

1st: "Ice cream and lemonade. Catch us if you're not afraid."

Then team one acts out some agreed-upon work, while team two guesses it. When the correct work is guessed, team two chases team one and tries to capture its players. A game with similar aspects is "Statues." The leader twirls each player around by one hand and lets him fly. As the children are released, they freeze in the position they land in, and the leader selects the best "statue" to be the next twirler. Both of these games have been very popular in Salt Lake City for the past several years, and probably much longer, for they have precedents among European children's games.

Game

Mrs. C. L. Wheeler
Salt Lake City
July 18, 1967

   After dinner every night the whole family would
sit around the large kitchen table. My father would
smoke his pipe, my mother would sew, and my sisters
and I would play a game with matches. You line up
ten match sticks in a straight line, and the object
is to take one match, skip two, and cross it; at the
end of the game you are to have all the matches
crossed. It really is harder than it sounds, and
we used to spend hours trying to do this right.

Margaret Anne Murphy

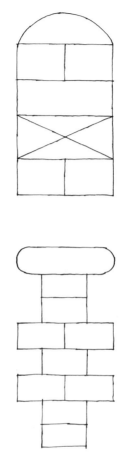

Most folk games are based on extremely simple, natural activities like running, jumping, chasing, hiding, fighting, or acting things out. The variations that creep into widespread games are often fairly minor, occurring perhaps just in the name of the game, other terms associated with it, order of play, local ground rules, or the like. The following describes a typical team game played with a ball around a building; in other regions it may be called "Anthony Over," "Eenie-I-Over," or something else. Notice how the local references to Utah mining towns where this version was played have crept in:

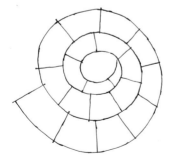

> *When I was a child we played a game we called "Andy I Over." There were four of us children who lived at the mine, so we usually had two on a side. Each one on a side would have his turn to throw the ball. We used a low building to throw the ball over, usually the garage across the road from my house, but sometimes we used the skip trestle or the rope house, which were really a challenge! As the ball was thrown over the building, the one throwing it would call, "Andy I Over," to warn the ones on the other side that it was coming. After the ball was thrown, the ones on the throwing side would try to run around the building before the others could catch the ball. If they succeeded, they got to throw the ball again, but if they didn't, the other side got to throw. When we used the trestle, or the rope house, we didn't try to run around, but whether we caught the ball or not was the game. The side that caught the ball the most times won. (Salt Lake City, 1967)*

Hopscotch is a universally played game in the U.S., sometimes regularized by adult authorities when the game diagram is painted permanently on a paved playground. But much more commonly the kind of diagram they like is redrawn in chalk by the children on a sidewalk or driveway each time they play. So far, seven variations have been reported from Utah and Idaho by student collectors.

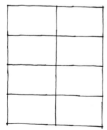

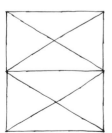

Hopscotch involves skillful tossing of the "taw" (rock, rubber heel, or other small object) and adroit hopping in and out of the proper squares of the diagram in the proper sequence. Other games played with equipment require even greater dexterity and motor skills. Mumblety peg and other knife games are based on accurately throwing a pocket knife from various positions and postures to make it stick in the ground. Various ball games in folk circulation develop the skills of hitting, pitching, catching, basket-shooting, or whatever. Jacks and marble games depend upon precise handling of small objects. Individual groups' elaborations on such games can sometimes reach surprising proportions. For instance, in one Salt Lake City elementary school recently pupils were observed playing a complex marble-gambling game they called "Hit It, You Get It." The game had a special terminology, rules, times and places of play, and customs. When a large portion of the schoolyard was used for many of these games going on at once, the whole picture began to resemble a Nevada casino in full swing. As the game escalated to playing for money, teachers had to step in to tone it down. In this case, children's play got too close to adult behavior for comfort.

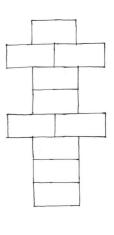

Many of the older books on folk games devoted much space to lamenting the loss of so many beautiful old children's singing and dramatic games. It is true that these have tended to be squeezed out, partly by Scout groups, television, Little League, and other organized recreations, and few children any longer play games like "Farmer in the Dell," "We Are Three Knights of Spain," or "Ring Around the Rosy." But if we accept, as we must, the modern children's own choices for play on their own terms, we will find them actively developing new folk games in imitation of the adult world. For instance, "plain" tag (which always had some variations) now can be played as "TV Tag," "Cigarette Tag," or "Vitamin Tag." Here is a child's own description:

> *When "It" comes toward you, you huddle up on the ground and let them trip over you, and if you're playing TV tag you have to say a show, like "Donna Reed." If it's Cigarette Tag, you say "Spring" or some other kind. For Vitamin Tag you have to say "Chox" and one of the colors, but not brown, black, or purple.*
>
> *(Salt Lake City, 1967)*

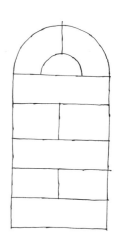

The customary pranks of occupations have already been mentioned, but two other kinds of pranks might also be noted. A favorite is the telephone prank: the faked message from a fictional caller:

> *One of the favorite office phone pranks is to leave a message for one of the staff to call Miss Liger, with her number listed after*

97

Photographed by Douglas Hill and William A. Wilson

Photographed by Douglas Hill and William A. Wilson

*the name. The "liger" is a beast unique to the Hogle Zoo in Salt
Lake City. It is a zoo-bred freak, half tiger, half lion. The message is
made to sound important so that the call is sure to be returned.
When the number is dialed, the answering voice says, "Hogle Zoo-
logical Gardens." Because most people don't think too fast, they
ask for Miss Liger. They are then told that she rarely leaves her
cage to answer the phone, or some other such remark. It's good for
a laugh, but I imagine Hogle Zoo gets tired of it.*

(Salt Lake City, 1968)

A second popular prank is the kind played at school: "One morning a teacher came into the room and found the following written as though from the other side of the blackboard, 'Help! I'm trapped behind this blackboard.'"

Here are some guides for collecting games in your own area:

Watch a group of children at play: what folk games do they play in what order? How do they choose "It" or the teams for the games?

Ask a child to list for you all the games he knows; how many are folk games?

Ask older people what traditional games, sports, or other recreations they had before TV.

Can you photograph any children playing folk games? Show them the pictures and write down their exact descriptions of how they play those games.

What local variations are there on baseball, basketball, and other organized sports?

Do the children in your area play any games with rhymes, chants, or songs in them?

Write down the entire vocabulary of jacks, marbles, or mumblety-peg.

Material Folk Culture

The material creations of folk culture are those things which are made in traditional ways and according to traditional designs either handed down from person to person or in imitation of other homemade artifacts. These folk objects may be houses and other buildings, fences and other utilitarian objects, tools, toys, tombstones, pottery, baskets, quilts, coverlets, costumes, foods, and in the realm of folk art, things decoratively braided, woven, stitched, whittled, sculptured, sketched, or painted. This is not a complete list, for no such list could be compiled without extensive collecting, and no such field work has been done yet in Utah, or indeed thoroughly in any part of the United States. Material folk culture is probably the greatest frontier left in American folklore research, and Utah's heritage promises to be one of the richest and most interesting of all.

As with many kinds of folklore, people tend to think of "folk art" in overly limited and stereotyped terms. A statue of Paul Bunyan, a family coat of arms, or a professionally painted piece of "Pennsylvania Dutch" furniture is taken for the real thing, which is assumed to be always quaint, lovely, and old fashioned. While it is true that most material folk culture *is* conservative, or "tradition-directed," there are, as with other kinds of folklore, plenty of examples of the on-going construction and use of folk objects. Furthermore, new variations on old items and even new items themselves continue to be developed. The collection of folk cultural material, then, is doubly a matter of recording the old and preserving a record of the current creations. The quest in such field work is not necessarily just for the beautiful and the romantic things, but more generally to document what the folk have taught each other to make from available materials to fill some of the real needs of their lives.

Here, for comparison, are two reports of children's folk creations from two recent folklore students at the University. The first describes the homemade dolls of her mother's generation, and the second concerns a school fad of only a few years ago. Both are based on simple pleasing designs, and they help fill the growing girl's need for play that is related to her coming role as wife and mother. The materials of both items, it should be noted, were common in the home and school.

Homemade Dolls   *Mrs. Ed. R. Smith*
                                    Salt Lake City
                                    May, 1968

Mrs. Smith, my mother, age sixty-five, spent her childhood in the San Juan area. Money was not readily available for playthings for children then, if the few commercial outlets had them at all. The fine dolls of the period were of the china variety, and not many of these found their way across the rugged country pioneered by my great grandmother and her generation. However, dolls were where you found them, and after the first year or two of settlement hollyhocks were found growing in many gardens. My mother said that they picked the blossoms, turned them upside down, and the pod formed the head of an imaginary doll dressed in a petal-colored ball gown. Occasionally, arms were formed by poking sticks through the flowers. Also, the old variety of clothespins were dressed, faces

101

painted on the head, and the fun began. Scraps of material, bits of thread or yarn formed wonderful products in the hands of small children.

Donna Gene Parker

Gum Wrapper Chains

Myself
Salt Lake City
November, 1969

When I was in junior high school all the girls caught on to the fad of making a chain out of gum wrappers. First we would undo one wrapper and tear it in half, folding each half into half twice lengthwise:

Then we would fold it from end to end, twice also:

102

When two were folded, we would push the ends of one through the spaces in the sides of the other:

The object of this was to keep adding to the chain until it was the same length as the height of the boy that you liked. Then you were supposed to light one end of it and if it burned all the way up the chain without going out, it meant that he liked you too.

Linda Messerly

A large part of the Utah folk heritage of material things may be easily observed right on the landscape. For this kind of collecting one does not need to begin by searching for informants; instead he can just wander about in small towns and across the countryside looking carefully at the things people have made for themselves and keeping track of the recurring patterns with notebook, sketchpad, or camera. Much of what one finds to report will depend on his knowing what to look for. For example, a trained cultural geographer studying the "Mormon village" in the summer of 1969, after examining some forty villages ranging in population from 400 to 1,000 inhabitants, outlined this typical description:

> . . . the Mormon village can be characterized as a spacious rural village, usually with wide streets, irrigation ditches, poplars, orchards, gardens, solid homes, barns and granaries right in town, and with old bleached fences made of almost anything available. The chapel is dominant in the scene. Towns such as Taylor and Joseph City, Arizona; Fayette, Scipio, Escalante, and Alpine, Utah; Lewisville and Franklin, Idaho, fit the description. (Quoted from Richard V. Francaviglia, "The City of Zion in the Mountain West," *The Improvement Era*, December, 1969, p. 17.)

The composite image of the Mormon village, this investigator determined, was formed partly from the city planning ideas of Joseph Smith and Brigham Young, and partly by transplanted forms and techniques from the home states of the settlers, modified by the special materials and needs on the frontier. The study of these typical patterns of development is done not to commend or imitate them for future villages, but to document and interpret the relationships between intellectual and practical aspects of a special American subculture. The same geographer, though neither a Utahn nor a Mormon, captured the spirit of daily life in many Utah small towns in these words:

> . . . the fact that a barn or pasture is visible from many parts of the city center definitely is characteristic of the Mormon village. Sheep may graze idly and horses lazily flick their tails, and more than one old barn can be seen — all from the steps of the post office or city hall. Many a Mormon parent has told me of the virtues of bringing up children "close to nature, with room to have fun."

But to other eyes, the same sights may be devoid of interest. In a letter to the editor of the *Salt Lake Tribune* (April 16, 1970), headlined "Rural Blight," an Ogden man commented, in part:

> There is a significant pollution problem in Utah that many people, apparently, are not concerned about. It is one of visual blight in the form of deteriorated barns, shacks, and fences in the rural sections of the state . . . eyesores that create an unfavorable image of our state with tourists and businessmen thinking of investing here. . . . Something needs to be done about old barns and fences. I suggest clearing them out, on a strictly volunteer basis, would be an ideal project for local church and civic organizations.

There are literally hundreds of kinds of folk things in countless variations to be collected, so it is well to begin with a general overview of your region and then narrow your search to one limited topic at a time. One good place to start is the farm or ranch site. How is the land divided for use? Where on the lot is the house built? What different materials were used in construction on older properties — adobe, earth, log, lumber, stone? For what use was each building made — barn, stable, granary, salt house, bunk house, well house, etc.? Which are still used for their original purposes and which have new functions or are abandoned? Make measured drawings of buildings and ask what the different parts or units were called. Make an inventory of the objects found in a typical barn or other building.

We refer here, of course, largely to the older folk-built structures. The old, partly destroyed, unpainted hay barn, for instance, interests us, or the log stable. Yet, if someone is building a new structure, it is well worth observing what traditional pattern or practice may be employed. A typical Utah granary, for instance, is built "inside-out," that is, with vertical studs on the outside and horizontal siding on the inside. With this design the pressure of grain inside keeps pressing the siding onto the studs instead of away from them as conventional construction would. The resulting structure, unpainted, undecorated, and weathered, with various "clutter" leaning up against it, is neither imposing nor attractive. Yet it did efficiently provide a good grain storage facility with tight smooth rodent and bird-proof walls inside and a minimum of corners there to catch loose grain. A superficial look at inside-out granaries of the region suggests that they tend to be about the same size and shape anywhere, but with a few notable exceptions. We need to have more data to generalize better. What are their dimensions? Where are they placed on the property? Describe the construction details. Where is the door or the filling opening placed? What other structures, if any, have inside-out construction? To what use are old granaries put when no longer used to store grain?

Besides the individual farm or ranch site, the whole smaller villages themselves should be given a bird's eye view. On a sketch map of the streets and alleys of a town, it is useful to mark with colors or symbols the location of civic buildings (in use or not) and all old houses, barns, granaries, and sheds. Not only does this provide a check sheet for the individual local collector to follow in his closer studies, but it gives the student of statewide patterns a good comparative look at his territory.

As we examine Utah folk cultural materials a bit more closely, we might want to focus next on house types. The houses were generally the first permanent structures erected in a settlement, and some very old houses still stand and indeed are still occupied in Utah. This does *not* mean, necessarily, log cabins. Almost any size and kind of house may have traditional aspects to it, and the study of their folk forms helps to plot the settlement patterns from East to West in the United States. Sometimes a sequence of houses may be reported from one site — the old dugout, followed by a cabin, and at last a large frame house. In such instances, residents should be interviewed and local records searched in order to determine as much of the history of the homestead as possible.

A small square or rectangular house built as one construction unit and only one or one-and-one-half stories tall is called a *cabin* by folklife scholars, of whatever

106

Photographed by Steven T. Walker

it is built. American cabins, which ultimately go back to English and Scotch-Irish cottage types, are either square or rectangular with a chimney at one gable end. If you find a cabin, you should sketch a measured floor plan, indicate the positions of doors, windows, and chimney, describe any additions (porch, lean-to shed, etc.), and draw or photograph the full front view and details of corner construction and window framing, especially on log cabins.

Larger traditional house forms are usually made of wood frame or stone in Utah. The most common design is the so-called "I" house or old "Nauvoo style" house. It is a tall two-story house with a chimney at each gable end and often a symmetrical arrangement of doors, windows, and gables at the front. Sometimes a larger home was constructed by putting two or three of these "I" houses together as an "L," "T," or even an "H." Another popular style is the lean-to or "Salt Box" house which is two stories in front sloping to one in back and often with a central chimney. Both of these are basic forms borrowed from the eastern United States and originally derived from Great Britain. To "collect" them, the main thing to do is get a clear photograph, sketch the floor plan, and note details such as construction material, interior divisions, cornerstone or other inscriptions, and the present condition, location, and ownership of the house. If your town has several interesting old homes with a similar traditional design expressed in one local material (such as sandstone), it may be that you could do some research on the local builders of a century or so ago and write a history of the prominent ones.

Before we leave the subject of housing, mention must be made of the two-front-door or "polygamy houses" of Utah. Since two-front-door houses are found elsewhere in the United States and many polygamous families involved more than just two wives, it seems doubtful that all the houses of this kind in Utah are authentically related to the practice of plural marriage. However, any such houses, or any other alleged "polygamy" construction in your community should be photographed or sketched and the legends surrounding it collected. (Another peculiar feature to inquire about is the second-story door that opens to blank space rather than a porch or balcony.)

Moving outside of houses, we should look at such important constructions as fences, gates, corrals and loading chutes, hay derricks, mail box stands, and any other homemade objects used to enclose and work the land. These too have their

108   Photographed by Jan Harold Brunvand

Nauvoo style or "I" house at Willard, Utah. The stone above the door bears the inscription "RJD 1861."

distinctive traditional forms and styles to document and classify. Fences, for example, may be easily devised from materials at hand, even the by-products of tilling the land. Ditches, hedges, or stone rows have sometimes served the purpose. Split rails may be turned into a picturesque, if somewhat wasteful, "Worm" (or "Zig Zag") fence, or the more efficient "Post and Rider," which has several variant forms. Juniper wood, rails, or tree roots may be woven together as a "Rip Gut" or

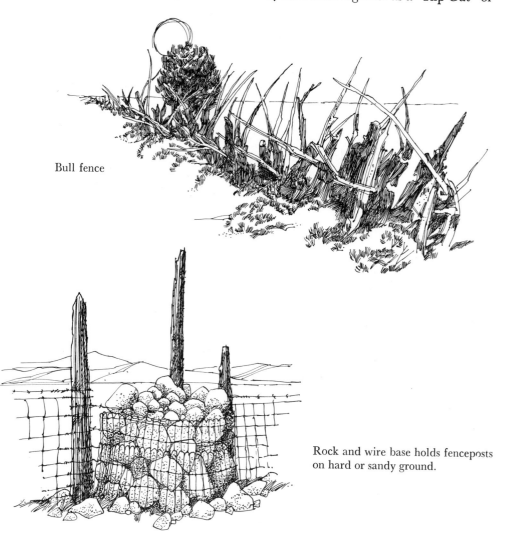

Bull fence

Rock and wire base holds fenceposts on hard or sandy ground.

110

"Bull" fence, and even willow branches can be stacked between posts to make a workable fence or corral. Besides the forms of fences themselves, it is interesting to learn about fence-construction procedures, hand signals used to line up fences, and local terms for fence types and parts. Even the partly commercial wire fences may have folk devices to brace or hold the wire and may have been erected by some traditional means. Gates, cattle guards, stiles, and any other improvements added to simple fencing should also be documented.

Willow fence

Rip gut fence

111

Hay derricks are a particularly distinctive feature of the rural Great Basin landscape, and should be, as a minimum, sketched in outline and spotted on a map. Any information about when and how and by whom a derrick was made is useful, and pictures of hay derricks in use are very valuable. Mail box stands, obviously, are a more recent folk craft, but already they have fallen into some traditional patterns, including the welded chain, rustic wood, wagon wheel, and pieces of discarded farm equipment such as plow, cream separator, or milk can. Wagon wheels, too, are used for fencing, gate construction, garden decorations, and sometimes chandeliers. Any such use of objects reminiscent of pioneering in Utah should be recorded.

Loading chute

Hay derrick

112

Many folk toys are still made of spools, paper, nuts and seeds, clothespins, flowers, burs, and other such materials; usually the techniques are passed from child to child rather than from adults to children. Some adults who can recall folk toys from their youth wrongly assume that these little crafts are lost nowadays; they fail to realize that today's children are often doing the very same things in their play:

> *When I was a little girl, my friends and I would pick dande-lions, pull off the flower and join the ends of the stems to make circles. Then we'd hook them all together and make a long chain.*
> *(Salt Lake City, 1969)*

Children fashion their simple toys from the supplies that come to hand in the kitchen, garage, or maybe father's workshop. Even a handful of old popsicle sticks may be used for a simple toy with an up-to-date name:

Folk toy   *Rick Carty*
                                                             Taylorsville
                                                             Summer, 1969

> *While I was working on the University of Utah grounds crew this summer, one of my working companions told me of a toy they used to make out of five popsickle sticks when he was a child. They called it a "flying saucer." The sticks were placed together in such a way that they were held together by tension. The children would throw them and make an accompanying exploding sound as it hit something. Being held together by tension, it would fly to pieces when it hit.*

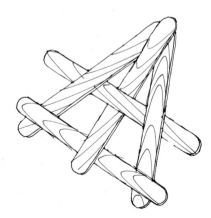

Jerry Stevenson   113

Smaller handcrafted things may next be surveyed. Here a major Utah item is the traditional quilt, or other sewn artifacts. These need to be documented in terms of the patterns, stitches, names, and the details of construction and transmission of the tradition. Is a quilt pattern passed down by drawing the design, showing a finished quilt, or perhaps by having a girl copy a block at a time from her mother's or grandmother's example? Are groups of girls introduced to quilting, or is it learned one by one?

Pottery, basketry, braiding, weaving, and whittling are all endeavors which overlap handicraft and folk art. That is, the products of these activities have both a direct utilitarian purpose and a distinct artistic appeal, as indeed may many of the materials we have been describing. Whittling, for instance, may be an activity just to while time away, doing nothing much more than reducing sticks to shavings. Or the whittler may make knickknacks, toys, whistles, or other devices for himself or others to use. Purely decorative whittling may be in the form of chains, ball-in-cage objects, or perhaps tiny baskets and other shapes carved from peach pits. Other than whittling one may study knot tying, buckskin and hair weaving, and other domestic crafts that combine artistic design and useful function.

Stonework in Utah, apart from building construction and decoration, is most prominent in tombstone art. The cemeteries of small towns and cities alike are rich sources of decorative and poetic tributes to the dead which tend to follow traditional themes — lambs and doves, flowers and vines, occupational symbols, reminders of the pioneer heritage, religious emblems, and the like. Tombstone art may be effectively collected either by "rubbing" it off with paper and crayon or photographing it. Even straight messages in words and statistics alone may contain interesting historical data, as in this example from the City Cemetery in Salt Lake City, complete with details of the death and containing contemporary spellings:

Sacred to the Memory of
Bishop, John Mills Woolley
Born Nov. 20th 1822
Chester County Pa.
Baptised Nauvoo Oct 7th 1840
Emigrated to Salt Lake Valley 1847

Stylized willow tree design from the back of a tombstone in Richfield. This design is sometimes called the "tree of life" motif.

From a rubbing by Mrs. Maury Haseltine

114

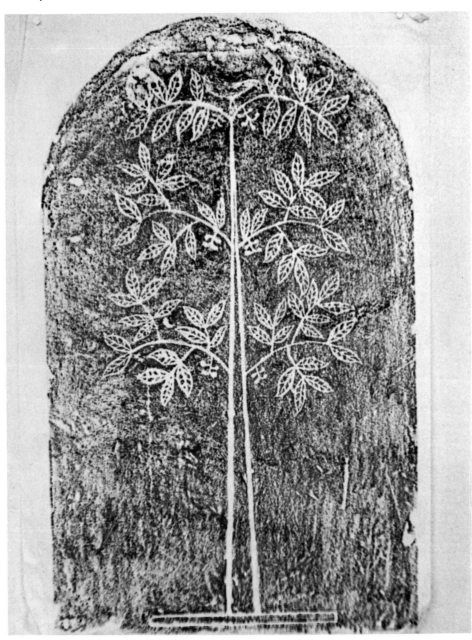

Photographed by Jan Harold Brunvand

Aspen tree carving of horse head using tree's scar tissue for mane.

Ordained bishop of the Ninth Ward
October 1856
Departed this Life
August 18th 1864
Occasioned by a blow from a rock
Driven by a Sliding log in
Little Cottenwood Kanyon.

S. L. Jones

(Note that the initials and surname of the artist are carved in the lower right hand corner.)

A recently noted folk art form common in Utah, but only scantily documented at present, is carving in the bark of Aspen trees. Though the Forest Service and other conservationists deplore this practice for the damage and defacement it wreaks on Aspen groves, the carving of names, initials, dates, designs, and pictures continues unabated. And, as ordinary as the mass of these carvings are, some efforts are truly artistic, exploiting as they do the ability of the living tree to restore the cut-away portion of the picture with black scar tissue in a few years. Examples have been photographed along the Wasatch Mountains of heart and leaf designs, elaborate inscriptions, and animal pictures skillfully carved on Aspens. Reports of other groups of carvings, probably done by lonely sheepherders, have come in from elsewhere in the state.

Utah, like most other states, has little in the way of folk costume tradition. (The exception is Pennsylvania with its distinctive "Dutch" — Amish, Mennonite, etc. — garb.) There is at least one costumed religious sect in Utah — the Sons of Aaron or "Levites" — and it would be useful to collect the history, details, and variations (if any) of their clothing. Otherwise, the only topics that suggest themselves are the possible distinctive dress of some occupations — sheepherding, cattle work, railroading, and the like. If there are any ethnic or regional clothing traditions in existence, we would like to know of them. Information about pioneer costume would also be welcome, as would data on ritual and ceremonial costumes of religious and fraternal groups.

Folk foods, our final topic in this *Guide*, have more possibility as a folklife subject than at first might be suspected in this age of the TV dinner and ready-mix

Photographed by Jan Harold Brunvand

Signature carving on an aspen tree on Dog Lake Trail, at the Millcreek-Brighton Divide near Salt Lake City. Such carvings by Frank and Tony Herrera are abundant along this trail.

dessert. Many housewives know recipes for "nothing-in-the-house" pies — substitutes, like seasoned cracker crumbs for the apples in a pie. There are traditional designs in some families to put into the top crust of a pie. Other folk foods may be gleaned from the wild plants of the land or based on the hunter's kills. Some are associated with holidays or other special events, and still others may be ethnic inheritances. Here are a few samples of folk foods taken from the student collections:

> *We used to make "ice cream" by pouring the cream skimmed from new milk over fresh but crusted snow. Add sugar and it tasted real good. (Salt Lake City, 1969)*
>
> *One of the favorite desserts of my family in Idaho is freshly picked lettuce, with sugar and cream. Fresh lettuce just isn't the same as store bought! (Salt Lake City, 1969)*
>
> *It was a standing tradition that on Christmas Eve my family would eat boiled potatoes topped with mounds of whipped cream. (Salt Lake City, 1969)*
>
> *To make "Sheepherder Potatoes," cook the onions together with the potatoes, about eight potatoes. Save one onion. Add one-eighth pound of butter, not margarine. Add salt and pepper. Boil till the potatoes and onions go mushy, not too mushy but real tender. They shouldn't be too dry. It's not a soup, but it's real moist. Serve it real hot. (Preston, Idaho, 1969)*
>
> *Grandpa's favorite was dandelion salad. He'd send you kids out with a sack and a knife and you'd dig dandelions. Then you'd clean them and cut off the pith and save the tender parts. This would make a large bowlful of greens. He'd cut up a small onion or garlic and add oil and vinegar and salt and pepper. His mother made this salad in Germany. We use the same recipe still, but we use lettuce instead of dandelions. (Salt Lake City, 1967)*

Finally, here is a complete recipe for a dish passed down in one Utah family. The description includes information about the traditional way to prepare the food and also about the transmission of it from one generation to another. It would make a good dish to snack on while reviewing this *Guide* and deciding what to begin collecting first:

Folk Food
                                             Mary E. Tassainer
                                             Salt Lake City
                                             November 15, 1967

118

> *Here is a recipe for German Apple Cake that has become a tradition in our family. Grandma Tassainer used to make this cake*

without a recipe and one day I got her to make the cake and I sat and wrote down everything she did and tried to get exact measures for the ingredients. All of the sons and daughters have her recipe but each recipe is different because each one got it the same way I did. I'll give you her recipe as she recited it to me and then I'll give you my version.

She'd have all the ingredients out on the table and start to work. A scoop of sugar, then some lard. She'd dip a spoon into the lard and look at it, decide it was enough and plop it into the bowl. Three eggs went in next and the mixture would be stirred until creamy. Then the dry ingredients. A sifter of flour, a pinch of salt. "About that much" baking powder, she'd say as she held some in the palm of her hand. A bit of mace for flavor. A capful of vanilla. And about "that much cream," she'd say and hold her thumb and forefinger about a half-inch apart.

After several trials and errors, I worked out this table of ingredients:

1 cup sugar	*2 squares butter or margerine*
3 eggs	*(better flavor than lard)*
pinch of salt	*4½ cups flour*
1 teaspoon mace	*2 teaspoons baking powder*
1 teaspoon vanilla	*½ cup milk or cream*

I put the cake together just the way she did.

The dough is very soft and pliable. Put it into greased pans, pushing it around with floured fingers to form a crust about ¼ inch thick. Be sure to cover the sides of the pan. Slice Jonathan or Roman Beauty apples very thin. Toss with generous amounts of sugar and cinnamon. Pour into dough lined pans. Roll some leftover dough thin and cut into strips. Make lattice work over top of apples.

Bake at 350 degrees until apples are tender (test with fork). Crust should be light brown. Remove from oven, and sprinkle generously with powdered sugar.

Alice Kaye Tassainer

Suggestions
for Further Reading

The best way to learn more about folklore and its study is to take one of the folklore courses available at all three major Utah universities. If this is not possible, a reader may get beyond the elementary stage represented by this volume by studying available scholarly publications. This *Guide* is similar in content and organization to the author's much longer and more comprehensive textbook *The Study of American Folklore: An Introduction* (New York, 1968) which contains voluminous bibliographies. Therefore, only a few recent general works and some items of special relevance to Utah folklore will be mentioned in this brief suggested reading list.

General Works:

A well-written collection of essays is *Our Living Traditions: An Introduction to American Folklore*, edited by Tristram P. Coffin (New York, 1968). The standard survey along historical lines remains Richard M. Dorson's *American Folklore* (Chicago, 1959). Dorson's regional anthology of texts *Buying the Wind: Regional Folklore in the United States* (Chicago, 1964) has a good section on Utah Mormon folklore, but a more detailed account is Austin E. and Alta Fife's *Saints of Sage and Saddle: Folklore Among the Mormons* (Bloomington, Ind., 1956).

Articles in professional journals (available in college and university libraries) dealing in a general way with the varieties of our regional folklore and its spirit are the following:

BAILEY, WILFRID. "Folklore Aspects in Mormon Culture," *Western Folklore*, 10 (1951), pp. 217–225.

BROOKS, JUANITA. "Memories of a Mormon Girlhood," *Journal of American Folklore*, 77 (1964), pp. 195–219.

BRUNVAND, JAN HAROLD. "Folklore of the Great Basin," *Northwest Folklore*, 3 (1968), pp. 17–32.

FIFE, AUSTIN E. "Folk Elements in the Formation of Mormon Personality," *Brigham Young University Studies*, 1–2 (1959–60), pp. 1–17.

Folksay:

The September 1968 issue of *Names*, journal of the American Name Society, was devoted to names and naming in folklore; the introductory essay by Jan Harold Brunvand scans the field and offers many examples, some of them from Utah folklore. Otherwise, none of the best studies and collections of folksay listed in *The Study of American Folklore* have been superseded. Perhaps the best single work on the subject is concerned with the many and various short verbal traditions known to English children — *The Lore and Language of Schoolchildren* by Peter and Iona Opie (Oxford and New York, 1959). Only three small collections of Utah folksay have been published:

LEE, HECTOR, and ROYAL MADSEN. "Nicknames of the Ephraimites," *Western Humanities Review*, 3 (1949), pp. 12–22.

WILSON, MARGUERITE IVINS. "O-U-T Spells Out: Some Counting-Out Rhymes of Utah Children," *Utah Humanities Review*, 2 (1948), pp. 310–318.

————. "Yours Till —: A Study of Children's Autograph Rhymes in Utah," *Utah Humanities Review*, 1 (1947), pp. 245–260.

Folk Literature:

The bibliography of American legends, folktales, ballads, and folksongs is enormous — each category and sub-category a study in itself. We can only list here the Utah items, which are fairly substantial, especially in the area of legend:

CANNING, RAY R. "Mormon Return-from-the-Dead Stories, Fact or Folklore," *Proceedings of the Utah Academy of Science, Arts, and Letters*, 42 (1965), pp. 29–37.

FERRON, RICHARD M. "Legendary Mining Men in Eastern Utah," *Utah Humanities Review*, 2 (1948), pp. 381–382.

FIFE, AUSTIN E. "The Legend of the Three Nephites Among the Mormons," *Journal of American Folklore*, 53 (1940), pp. 1–49.

――――. "Popular Legends of the Mormons," *California Folklore Quarterly*, 1 (1942), pp. 105–125.

HAND, WAYLAND D. "The Three Nephites in Popular Tradition," *Southern Folklore Quarterly*, 2 (1938), pp. 123–129.

LEE, HECTOR. *The Three Nephites: The Substance and Significance of the Legend in Folklore.* Albuquerque, N.M., 1949.

WILSON, WILLIAM A. "Mormon Legends of the Three Nephites Collected at Indiana University," *Indiana Folklore*, 2 (1969), pp. 3–35. (Not collected in Utah, but closely related to Utah tradition.)

Besides Lester A. Hubbard's *Ballads and Songs from Utah* (Salt Lake City, 1961) and Thomas E. Cheney's *Mormon Songs from the Rocky Mountains: A Compilation of Mormon Folksong* (Austin, Tex., 1968), folksongs are often included in the Daughters of Utah Pioneers collections *Heart Throbs of the West* (1939–). Utah folksongs in folklore journals include the following:

BURT, OLIVE WOOLLEY. "Murder Ballads of Mormondom," *Western Folklore*, 18 (1959), pp. 141–156.

DAVIDSON, LEVETTE J. "Mormon Songs," *Journal of American Folklore*, 58 (1945), p. 273–300.

FIFE, AUSTIN E., and ALTA S. FIFE. "Folk Songs of Mormon Inspiration," *Western Folklore*, 6 (1947), pp. 42–52.

Folklife:

Customary traditions are occasionally well collected, but generally little interpreted in American folklore. *The Study of American Folklore* lists what there is. For a really thorough discussion, say, of children's games, we must turn again to an English work, Peter and Iona Opie's *Children's Games in Street and Playground* (Oxford and New York, 1969). A brilliant presentation and analysis of the material traditions of another region is Henry Glassie's *Pattern in the Material Folk Culture of the Eastern United States* (Philadelphia, 1968). Logan, Utah, was the site in 1968 of a pioneering conference on western folklife from which emerged in the USU Monograph Series a collection edited by Austin E. and Alta Fife and

Henry Glassie entitled *Forms Upon the Frontier: Folklife and Folk Arts in the United States* (Logan, 1969); included are discussions of Utah houses, fences, tombstones, Aspen tree carvings, costumes, and several other topics.

Custom and belief in Utah are treated in the following items:

CHENEY, THOMAS E. "Utah Courtship Customs," *Western Folklore*, 19 (1960), p. 106.

FIFE, AUSTIN E. "Folk Belief and Mormon Cultural Autonomy," *Journal of American Folklore*, 61 (1948), pp. 19–30.

————. "Folkways of the Mormons from the Journals of John D. Lee," *Western Folklore*, 21 (1962), pp. 229–246.

————. "Pioneer Mormon Remedies," *Western Folklore*, 16 (1957), pp. 153–162.

NOALL, CLAIRE. "Superstitions, Customs, and Prescriptions of Mormon Midwives," *California Folklore Quarterly*, 3 (1944), pp. 102–114.